UNSOLVED MURDERS
IN SOUTH YORKSHIRE

TRUE CRIME FROM WHARNCLIFFE

Foul Deeds and Suspicious Deaths Series

Barking, Dagenham and
    Chadwell Heath
Barnet, Finchley and Hendon
Barnsley
Bath
Bedford
Birmingham
Black Country
Blackburn and Hyndburn
Bolton
Bradford
Brighton
Bristol
Cambridge
Cardiff
Carlisle
Chesterfield
Colchester
Cotswolds
Coventry
Crewe
Croydon
Cumbria
Derby
Doncaster
Dublin
Durham
Ealing
Fens
Folkestone and Dover

Glasgow
Grimsby and Cleethorpes
Guernsey
Guildford
Halifax
Hampstead, Holburn and
    St Pancras
Huddersfield
Hull
Isle of Wight
Islington
Jersey
Kensington and Chelsea
Leeds
Leicester
Lewisham and Deptford
Liverpool
London's East End
London's West End
Manchester
Mansfield
More Foul Deeds Barnsley
More Foul Deeds Birmingham
More Foul Deeds Chesterfield
More Foul Deeds Wakefield
Newcastle
Newport
Norfolk
Northampton
Nottingham

Oxfordshire
Pontefract and Castleford
Portsmouth
Reading
Richmond and Kingston
Rochdale
Rotherham
Scunthorpe
Sheffield
Shrewsbury and Around
    Shropshire
South Yorkshire
Southampton
Southend-on-Sea
Southport
Staffordshire and the Potteries
Stratford and South
WarwickshireSuffolk
Swansea
Tees
The Fens
Uxbridge
Wakefield
Warwickshire
West Riding of Yorkshire
Wigan
Worcester
York
Yorkshire Coast

OTHER TRUE CRIME BOOKS FROM WHARNCLIFFE

Black Barnsley
Brighton Crime and Vice 1800–2000
Britain's Most Notorious Hangmen
Crafty Crooks and Conmen
Criminal Women
DNA Crime Investigations
Durham Executions
Enemies of the State
Essex Murders
Executions & Hangings in Newcastle & Morpeth
Great Hoaxers, Artful Fakers and Cheating
    Charlatans
Great Train Crimes
Hanged in Lancashire
Kent Murder and Mayhem
Jack the Ripper: Quest for a Killer
Miscarriages of Justice
Murder and Mayhem in North London
Norfolk Mayhem and Murder
Norwich Murders
Notorious Murders of the Twentieth Century
Rotherham Murders
Scotland Yards's Ghost Squad
Serial Killers: Butchers and Cannibals

Serial Killers: Murder Without Mercy
Serial Killers: The World's Most Evil
Strangeways: A Century of Hangings in
    Manchester
The A-Z of London Murders
The Guv'nors
The Plot to Kill Lloyd George
The Romford Outrage
The Sweeney
The Thames Torso Murders
The Wharncliffe A-Z of Yorkshire Murder
Unsolved East Anglian Murders
Unsolved London Murders: The 1920s and 1930s
Unsolved London Murders: The 1940s and 1950s
Unsolved Murders in and Around Derbyshire
Unsolved Murders in Victorian & Edwardian
    London
Unsolved Norfolk Murders
Unsolved Yorkshire Murders
War Crimes
Warwickshire's Murderous Women
Yorkshire's Hangmen
Yorkshire's Multiple Killers
Yorkshire's Murderous Women

Please contact us via any of the methods below for more information
or a catalogue
WHARNCLIFFE BOOKS
47 Church Street, Barnsley, South Yorkshire, S70 2AS
Tel: 01226 734555 • 734222 • Fax: 01226 734438
email: enquiries@pen-and-sword.co.uk
website: www.wharncliffebooks.co.uk

UNSOLVED MURDERS IN SOUTH YORKSHIRE

Real Life Cold Cases of the Nineteenth and Twentieth Centuries

SCOTT C. LOMAX

First Published in Great Britain in 2013 by
Wharncliffe Books
an imprint of
Pen and Sword Books Ltd.
47 Church Street
Barnsley
South Yorkshire
S70 2AS

Copyright © Scott C. Lomax 2013

ISBN: 978-1-84563-159-8

Typeset in 11/13pt Plantin by Concept, Huddersfield.

Printed and bound in England by
CPI Group (UK) Ltd, Croydon, CR0 4YY

Pen & Sword Books Ltd incorporates the Imprints of Pen & Sword Aviation, Pen & Sword Family History, Pen & Sword Maritime, Pen & Sword Military, Pen & Sword Discovery, Wharncliffe Local History, Wharncliffe True Crime, Wharncliffe Transport, Pen & Sword Select, Pen & Sword Military Classics, Leo Cooper, The Praetorian Press, Remember When, Seaforth Publishing and Frontline Publishing.

For a complete list of Pen & Sword titles please contact
PEN & SWORD BOOKS LIMITED
47 Church Street
Barnsley
South Yorkshire
S70 2BR
England
E-mail: enquiries@pen-and-sword.co.uk
Website: www.pen-and-sword.co.uk

Contents

Acknowledgements

would like to thank the staff at Sheffield Local Studies Library for the access to newspaper archives and for permission to use historic photographs from the Picture Sheffield collection. I would also like to thank David Clifford Taylor for his knowledge of many unsolved murders which helped me identify some of the cases featured in this book and proved to be a useful starting point in my research. I would like to thank my wife for her support and for accompanying me on some very long walks across South Yorkshire to take photographs and carry out research.

Finally I would like to thank Sue Blackhall, Lisa Hooson and all of the staff at Pen and Sword Books who have assisted in the production of this book.

Introduction

'Truth will come to light, murder cannot be hid long, a man's son may, but at the length truth will out' said Launcelot in *The Merchant of Venice*. Whilst the passage of time can, and has, uncovered many secrets, killers could get away with their crimes in 1596 when Shakespeare penned these words and this is certainly the case in more recent times as the following chapters clearly demonstrate.

Most murders today are quickly solved. Often the perpetrator is caught red-handed or they are easily found out because most murders take place in the home by someone known to the victim, and so the number of suspects is limited. Many murders are not particularly well planned, sometimes being spur of the moment actions, and so evidence is quickly obtained to identify the culprit. There is also CCTV footage available for most urban centres and an increasing number of businesses and residential areas. Furthermore, some groups of people who were historically unwilling to speak to the police are now more cooperative. Improved scientific techniques and policing methods have also helped, of course.

Despite improved investigation tools and methods too many criminals are escaping justice. In 1999 the Macpherson Report into the Metropolitan Police Force's handling of the original investigation into the murder of Stephen Lawrence claimed the national average murder detection rate was 92 per cent – i.e. eight out of 100 murders were going unsolved. This proportion was exactly the same in 2008–9 according to figures from the Ministry of Justice. So unsolved murders remain a problem, with improved forensic techniques not reducing the proportion of unsolved cases, at least in part because there is not always compelling forensic evidence left at a crime scene. There can be no doubt, of course, that forensic science has resulted in countless convictions where forensic evidence is present, but even in this advanced technological age people are getting away with murder. What was the situation like before any advanced forms of forensic examination was conceived, even before DNA testing, and before other tools used by modern police forces?

In cases where there was little or no evidence to identify a suspect or prove their guilt the victim is denied justice. Friends and relatives of the victim obviously suffer as they continue to wonder why their loved one was killed, and by whom, and this pain continues throughout their lives. Society as a whole also suffers because a murderer continues to live in its midst, free to commit further crime and this often puts enduring fear into communities.

The following chapters are examples of such cases. The early chapters include cases of historic interest where killers certainly went to their graves in the knowledge they had got away with murder. Cases include suspicious deaths which left detectives in South Yorkshire baffled, but which were, it would seem, acts of callous murder which were not recognised as such due to dubious police opinions and practices. There are also cases of clear murder such as a man shot in the head during the Victorian period, whose killer was never identified.

The later chapters, however, feature cases where there is still the possibility that the wicked men or women who were responsible for such acts of inhumanity may remain within our society. These include a man murdered for less than £70 in a city centre multi-storey car park, a teenage girl abducted, sexually assaulted and left dead at the foot of a dung hill, a young mother who entered prostitution and died at the hands of a man with more than sex on his mind, a disabled woman who was strangled in her home which was then set ablaze, and a newborn baby girl whose body was found in the toilets of a shop in Barnsley.

For some of these cases there is the chance that someone has information which, despite the passage of decades, could lead to one or more individuals standing trial for murder. Justice can still prevail.

Over the years while I have been writing about murders many people have claimed my interest is somewhat dark. There has always been a fascination for me about mysteries of the present and past and I know this is shared by many others who I am sure will be as fascinated when reading about the cases old, and not so old, featured in this book, as I was researching and writing about them.

However, the following pages are intended to serve a further purpose in addition to satisfying fascination. When writing about unsolved cases of the past I believe that it is as important today to write about these cases as it was back when the crimes were committed and journalists were writing anything and everything they could about the crimes. I want to send out a clear message in the following pages to those killers – some of whom most likely still live in South Yorkshire – who committed evil acts decades ago. With the passage of time these criminals may well have begun to relax and gain somewhat normal lives. They may have children and grandchildren and try to lead respectable lives believing they have got away with murder. I want these people to know that they should continue to look over their shoulders, that they are not safe, that there are people still looking for them and I want them to be prepared to be found. I want to make sure these people have fear in their minds for what they have done, until that day when they are caught or when they take their secrets to their grave.

Snig Hill Police Station, the headquarters of South Yorkshire Police. (The author)

Whilst the police say they never give up searching for murderers – and there is clear evidence of their determination in some of the chapters which follow, most notably the murder of Anne Dunwell – there is a need for more appeals for information in order to maintain public interest and to ensure that cases are not forgotten. When cases are forgotten information ceases to be obtained. I hope that this book will renew interest and hopefully lead to new information.

I believe that by reminding people of crimes sometimes forgotten, new information can come to light. My book *Unsolved Murders in and Around Derbyshire* generated a large amount of new information, including the names of potential suspects for six of the 12 cases. This information is, at the time of writing, being reviewed by the police. It is my hope that the following chapters generate the same, if not a greater, response.

Let us hope that Shakespeare's words will prove correct and that in the case of some of the following cases the truth will out.

CHAPTER 1

A Victorian Shooting: The Murder of George Firth (1851)

It was shortly before 6am on Friday, 24 January 1851, that miners George Bostwick and Moses Armitage set off to the Eastfield Colliery where they both worked. As part of the journey they had to cross some fields at Berry Moor However, as they started to go down a slope something diverted them from their ordinary routine. Even in the darkness the two men could see a figure lying on the ground. As they approached and looked closely they realised it was a man lying on his left side with his feet on the footpath and his head towards the slope. His cap lay nearby on his right side. It was covered in blood (unnoticeable in the darkness). The man was not identifiable at first because of the poor light, but Armitage later recognised him as George Firth who lived approximately 100 yards away.

George was a 42-year-old bachelor who lived alone in a cottage in a small hamlet known as Partridge Dale or Berry Moor Bottom in the town of Thurgoland between Barnsley and Penistone, and which was in the heart of the Silkstone coalfield. The cottage was close to Holling Dyke pit which belonged to George's father, Joseph, who lived at Peel Street in Barnsley. Joseph also owned the Partridge-dale pit and was a joint partner of Victoria Colliery. Firth worked as a banksman at Holling Dyke, but occasionally assisted in the management of the pit.

George was conscious but was in a state of insensibility. The men did not believe there were any grounds for concern and believed that George was simply drunk as his drinking habit was well known to Armitage and the community at large. And they did not notice the pool of blood in which he lay, or the wound to the back of his head from which blood still poured. They asked

George to get up, to which he responded 'Ay, ay', but he remained on the ground and made no effort to move. The men stood him up, put his cap on his head and managed to drag him along between them. They later said that between them they 'paddled' him the very short distance home. George was completely incapable of walking and gave no sensible conversation. En route George did recognise one of those assisting him and exclaimed 'Oh holloa Sam!' before returning to his silence.

When they arrived at George's cottage he was unable to find his key and had to ask Armitage to get it from his pocket. Armitage then unlocked the door, assisted George into the building, and at his request, laid him down on a long settle. After a few moments George instructed the two men to leave, saying, 'You may go now. I shall manage.' Already late for work the two men did as requested and made their way to the colliery. Even now the men had no reason to believe that George was anything but drunk which the reader will soon discover was quite remarkable.

George's next-door neighbour Sarah Hague was at home when George was brought back and heard his arrival and the departure of the two men. Approximately an hour afterwards she heard the sound of something heavy falling. The sound clearly originated from next door and so she immediately went round to the cottage where she found George on the floor, having fallen off the settle. She lit the fire after asking his permission and then raised his head – only to be alarmed at the large quantity of blood that had formed beneath him. George asked for some water which he was given, together with a bottle of beer Hague found in the room. She then called another neighbour, Mary Perry, for assistance. Other neighbours arrived when they realised there was an injured man in need of assistance. George began to complain about a pain in his head, saying it was 'all in a puddle' which the women did not understand. George could not explain how he had come to be injured but did mention something about 't'steps', perhaps referring to the seven or eight steps which formed the stile and which were eight yards from where he was found. By this time his cap, clothing, the long settle and the floor were heavily covered in blood. As one neighbour, Charles Sidens, cleaned George's head wound, George said he had fallen off some steps. He then once again became silent and medical assistance was sought.

John Thomas B. Ellis, a surgeon from Silkstone, arrived between 10am and 11am, at which time George was conscious but in bed. Ellis noticed that in addition to the serious head wound, the injured man had a contused upper lip, contusions on the right eye and a scratch on one side of his face which was deep enough to be referred to as a 'laceration'. Whether these were caused by a fight or a fall was uncertain, and George did not give any useful information about how he came to be injured. Ellis concluded that George had fallen backwards due to intoxication and then cracked his head on an edge of one of the stone steps. Prior to leaving, Ellis asked his patient how the injuries were sustained, and again George simply said 'the steps'. Ellis tried to treat the wounds and sent for some ointment to put on them. This could only ease the suffering of the injured man, for it was already accepted that George was dying, and so Ellis did not return to offer further treatment. Indeed, George died the following morning at around 6am. His mother had been present from the day he was brought home and was with him when he died. She had asked her son many times how he came to be injured but he said he did not know.

Newspaper articles reported how the scene was visited by everyone in the neighbourhood – highlighting the characteristic curiosity that leads people to view the scenes of any violent murder or other death. A small pool of blood where George was found was particularly well viewed. Whilst there was blood eight yards from the steps there was no blood on the steps themselves to explain the injuries, and although doubts about the original theory were raised, death was still initially considered to be the consequence of a drunken accident.

The inquest was held on Tuesday 28 January at Mr Jonas Hague's home, the Eastfield Inn at Hollin Moor, near the scene of the crime. The coroner presiding over the inquest was Thomas Badger. Identification evidence as to who the victim was and an account of George's last known movements were presented before the inquest was adjourned. But the coroner requested that a post-mortem examination be undertaken to establish the cause of death

Any thoughts that George had fallen and smashed his head on the steps were shown to be highly erroneous when the post-mortem examination was undertaken on 29 January, three days after George had breathed his last. It was carried out by John Ellis who was assisted by his brother, Edwin, and a surgeon named

Mr T. Wainwright. John Ellis, who had at first believed George died following an accident whilst drunk, was startled when he found a flattened bullet which had been a lead slug or ball, above the right eye behind the frontal bone. The bullet had been fired from behind, with the wound at the back of the head. The bullet had passed through the brain in a downward direction shattering the skull; pieces of which were found embedded in the brain. A large effusion of blood was also found on the brain – part of which was protruding from what was now clearly a gunshot wound. There was also a fracture on the right-hand side of the head which was large enough to insert the tip of a finger into. A second wound might also have been caused by a gunshot, but this was unlikely. Death was caused by the single gunshot wound and the consequential loss of blood. It was really quite remarkable that George had managed to live for so long after being shot and that he should fail to even realise that he *had* been shot.

It was apparent therefore, that George had been shot at least once as he crossed over the stiles. Perhaps the killer was hidden. Certainly George did not know he had been shot and almost certainly did not see his assailant. It is almost certain that he would have lost consciousness immediately or almost instantaneously. He may also have fallen off the steps, possibly as a result of being shot, and acquired the scratch and other minor injuries at that time. But it could not be ruled out that he was struck by his assailant during a struggle, although his lack of knowledge about what had happened made this highly unlikely. It is also possible he fell from the steps and was on the ground when shot.

Traces of gunpowder were found in George's hair around his wound, and also on his cap, which showed that an airgun had not been used. (It was originally thought that an airgun was used because no one had reported hearing a gunshot.) A woman who lived around 200 yards from where George was found was awake between 1am and 2am (presumably during which time George was shot unless he was significantly delayed in his walk home), waiting for a lodger to return, but had heard no sound. (The lodger did not in fact return home that night as the reader will soon learn.) However, there need not have been a loud sound from the gun if the barrel was touching or very close to George's head when the shot was discharged. It could also be that those living in the area were not woken by the sound. No one lived within 100 yards of the location where George was found and so the sound may not have been heard.

There was no evidence that George had been robbed. He had five pennies and a halfpenny on his person, probably all of the money left after buying drinks that night. This is not to say he was not the victim of an intended robbery which had gone wrong, with his killer having panicked and fled empty-handed, but it seems unlikely. The most plausible scenario was that he was shot by someone who knew him and who had a grievance against him.

John Firth, George's 25-year-old brother who worked as an engine tender at Victoria Colliery and lived with his father in Peel Street, said he had been drinking with his sibling. He informed the inquest that George had been on a drinking binge for several days and had been drunk on the night before his body was found. There was no doubt that the deceased had been an alcoholic prone to heavy drinking sessions. The two brothers had been to Robinson's ale house until around 11pm and then headed to Dodworth. John claimed he had last seen his brother late that night when they stood opposite Dodworth chapel and George began swearing loudly as he lit his pipe with Lucifer matches. Allegedly, two young men dressed in jackets and caps approached them and told George to be quiet, to which George replied 'Go to Hell'. John said he told them to leave and to ignore George on account of him simply being drunk. He added that one of the two men had a gun. After ten minutes, at approximately 12.30am, George set off for the four-mile journey to his home, heading in the direction to which the two men had earlier walked. John told the inquest that George was capable of walking, adding that there had been no quarrel between him and his brother. If John was telling the truth this would make the two men strong suspects.

The inquest was resumed on the Wednesday following the post-mortem, to allow for the medical evidence to be heard. Adjourning the inquest again to allow for further police investigations, Badger announced he would write to the Home Secretary, Sir George Grey, to request a government reward for information leading to a conviction. There was, however, a development very soon after the adjournment without the necessity of a reward which would lead to a man standing trial for George Firth's murder.

John Firth was arrested at around 10pm on the night of 29 January on suspicion of murdering, or being involved in the murder of his

Dodworth Chapel, where George Firth and his brother John stood outside after leaving the Gate Inn. (The author's collection)

brother. The arrest was made by Superintendent William Green of Barnsley. Following his arrest John was described as being very low spirited and he repeatedly protested his innocence.

It was speculated that John had killed his brother for financial gain because although George spent almost all of the money he had on drink, John told the police that the collieries were doing well. It was therefore believed he may have killed his brother for a larger share of any profits.

Other early lines of enquiry related to George's colleagues at the colliery because it was claimed he had been domineering towards the workers and may have made enemies as a consequence. Those who had known George, however, claimed he was an honest and inoffensive man but affected by alcohol to which he had become addicted. The police favoured the theory of fratricide (the killing of a brother).

At the resumed inquest at the Wortley Arms on the Thursday following George's death, John Firth was represented by Mr Tyas, a Barnsley-based solicitor. Eliza Firth gave evidence that on the day her brother was shot John had returned home at around 1.30am or 2am. She was not aware that either of her brothers owned a gun. There was plenty of evidence, however, showing that John *had* indeed owned a gun. The court was told that he had a 'stick gun' nine or ten years previously and had owned one until shortly before the shooting of his brother.

Other evidence relating to the gun was forthcoming. John Haynes, a blacksmith, said that around three years earlier he had been asked to repair a walking stick gun belonging to the accused. There was also further evidence for John having a gun at the time of his brother's murder. John Sugden, a collier at Victoria Colliery, told the inquest that when he went to work on the 23 January he saw John in the smith's workshop filing something. When questioned about what he was doing John eventually admitted, 'Yes, it is something like a pistol. It is something to shoot with.' He told Sugden that it was a walking stick gun he was working on. Samuel Exley, a Barnsley gunsmith, said that before Christmas John had brought an old walking stick for him to repair and collected it in early January.

Another employee, Joseph Marsland, corroborated Sugden's story. He saw John Firth cutting a piece of sheet lead to produce two pieces of lead which he then fitted to the barrel of the stick gun.

In December, according to William Simpson the blacksmith at Victoria Colliery, he had made around twenty lead bullets at John Firth's request. John had provided the blacksmith with lead, a ladle and a mould, and as payment for making the bullets Simpson had been allowed to keep half of those he made. On 4 January John brought him a walking stick gun to repair. John told the blacksmith that he was intending to sell it. Simpson fitted an iron knob to one end of it and carried out some simple repairs.

Joseph Firth, George and John's father, informed the inquest that George had been a drunkard for approximately twenty years. He said that John had a walking stick gun a few weeks earlier, before Christmas, and that John was intending to sell it. John had told his father that the gun had been stolen from his cabin, but this revelation was only made two days after the shooting which many could be forgiven for thinking was too much of a coincidence to be truthful.

Further doubt about John's story was provided by workers who saw John working on the gun on the evening before George was found dying. At between 6pm and 7pm he was seen carrying out some work on the firearm in a workshop.

When John's home was searched by Superintendent Green on 29 January, John reiterated his claim about the two men who had approached him and George as they stood across from the chapel, one of whom he claimed had a gun. John also told the policeman that he had left his brother after the drinking session because he had forgotten to put the damper down at the colliery. He returned to the colliery in order to do this, he claimed, before heading home where he arrived at around 2am.

The claim of forgetting to put down the damper later raised suspicions in the minds of some of John's colleagues. They informed the police that it was practice to put down the damper at the end of the working day and that it was such habitual behaviour that it could not be forgotten. Colliery manager James Lawton, suggested that it *was* possible to forget – but that even if a worker did forget to carry out this task it would have been unnecessary to return because it would only delay work by half an hour the following morning if it had not been put down. Was John lying about this to provide a false account of his movements? Or could he have had concerns of any consequences to his work, perhaps exacerbated by alcohol, if the damper had been left up?

John also informed Green that his own gun had been stolen from the engine house at Victoria Colliery shortly before the shooting. No gun was found at John's home during the search. Had it been stolen or did John dispose of it after shooting his brother?

Could John's gun have been stolen by one of his colleagues who then went on to kill George? It seemed a far-fetched scenario. Doubts about John's story were increased when it was discovered he had tried to have evidence destroyed. It emerged that on the morning of Wednesday 29 January when Green was searching the house, a highly agitated John asked John Hutchinson, the book-keeper at Victoria Colliery, to go and tell Simpson to destroy any remaining bullets that he had. He protested his innocence and again gave his account of having left his brother at around 12.30am in order to put the damper down at the colliery before reaching home at around 2am. Hutchinson discussed the matter with some friends, including a Mr Piggott, and decided not to tell Simpson.

Instead, Piggott went to the police with the information and spoke to Superintendent Green. It was also discovered that on the day after George's death John had asked Simpson if he still had any of the bullets. 'If I were thee I would get shut of them, or they will get thee into a hobble,' the blacksmith was told.

A constable named William White searched a sewer on 6 February in the hope of finding evidence. His search was fruitful when he discovered seven lead bullets which were of the same iron and arsenic type as the slug recovered from George. This did not mean that John was responsible, but it seemed to suggest his weapon and the bullets made at his request were used to kill his brother. It later transpired that the bullets had been disposed of by Simpson's wife. An extensive search failed to locate John's gun. (Unfortunately, no information could be found during my research about where the sewer was located or the circumstances which led to the sewer being searched.)

There was no evidence of a quarrel between the two brothers, or any animosity between them. George Twigger of Berry Brow had accompanied the two brothers at The Gate pub on Dodworth Road. He was the lodger referred to earlier, but he did not return home that night because he was suffering from a bad back. He stayed instead at his brother's home in Dodworth. John had finished work at some time after 7pm and was later seen outside The Gate pub at between 8pm and 9pm, at which time George was drinking in Barnsley. Their father was heading back to Barnsley, from the market, accompanied by two men and said to his companions, 'Let us go into The Gate and have a glass', but John advised them not to, saying, 'You had better not go into The Gate inn.' John, Joseph and the two men headed towards Barnsley where they met George who was with Twigger. The brothers returned to The Gate and Twigger soon joined later, with three others accompanying them for some time, leaving John and George stood outside at around 11.30pm. The landlord of the pub, William Robinson, informed the inquest that the two brothers had called into the pub on that Thursday night and were present for around three quarters of an hour, with George being evidently drunk, whilst John appeared much more sober. He had refused to serve George any more ale which is why the brothers left. There had been no quarrel during their visit. The brothers consumed a quart of ale and bought a pennyworth of tobacco. Neither Twigger, any of the other men, nor Robinson observed John with any form of gun and certainly nothing resembling a stick gun or even a stick. As the brothers left The Gate they were seen talking pleasantly to one another.

The inquest heard that John would not look at his brother's body when he went to view it with his father at the cottage the day after George's death. This was used as evidence of his guilt. He accepted he was a suspect and agreed with Mrs Perry that people would think he was guilty as he was the last to be seen with his brother. John, his father, Perry and others visited the site where George was found. Whilst walking to the field John had lingered behind and again told Perry that people might say he committed the murder before running home. However, at this point in time it had not been established that George had been murdered. It was still believed that he had died as a result of a drunken accident, so why would John be concerned that he would be blamed for his brother's death?

At the inquest, John privately asked Constable White about his prospects of execution if he was committed to trial at York and convicted of his brother's murder. He wondered if there was any possibility he would be transported to Australia. He also asked the constable whether he could think of any example of where a man had been found guilty of murdering his brother or convicted on the grounds of little evidence. The constable told the accused that he had indeed come across some instances of convictions on the basis of questionable evidence and that a man named Dyon had been convicted of shooting his brother which had led to Dyon and a nephew of the victim being hung. A lengthy discussion took place between the men about the alternative verdicts which could be reached, and their likelihood.

Were these the ramblings of a guilty man trying to determine his fate or could they have been the concerns of an innocent man who believed he could be wrongly convicted?

He also asked White for some paper, on which he produced a drawing of his gun which he once again claimed had been stolen but was being repaired on the night before of George's murder. He said he then left it under the floor of the engine house where the tallow and pit rope were kept. He added that a round thing, like an apple in shape, had also been stolen.

The inquest jury was not convinced of John's guilt despite what in many other cases may have been seen to be compelling evidence.

He was, after all, the last person to see George alive, had owned a gun such as that used to kill his brother, and had made repairs to it shortly before the murder. His claims that the gun was stolen could not be substantiated. Perhaps, then, the fact that John was not seen to be in possession of that large gun when seen drinking with his brother on the night of the shooting, plus the lack of any incriminating remark from the deceased, was sufficient to cast doubt about the police theory. However, even if John was not in possession of the gun when seen on the night of 23/24 January could he not have hidden it somewhere nearby and retrieved it in order to commit his crime? John was discharged at the inquest due to the doubts. However, the police remained convinced of his guilt and so he was apprehended again, charged with the murder and indicted to stand trial at the York Assizes.

Despite the police's belief in John's guilt, the accused man had some grounds for optimism. Given that the inquest jury had not declared he was guilty when returning their verdict, Constable White believed that it was unlikely that John would be executed if found guilty at his murder trial. During a conversation with the constable, John informed the police officer that he wanted to get his affairs in order in the event of a guilty verdict. He believed he would be transported to Australia and wanted to ensure that should he be allowed to return to England, he did not want to ever work again.

The case had drawn tremendous interest, resulting in a packed courtroom when the trial opened at the York Assizes in March 1851. Those who had gathered to watch found John to be respectably dressed in black and heard him enter a not guilty plea in a low but firm voice. It was remarked upon in the press of the day that throughout the trial John Firth gave an air of confidence and collectedness. He was provided with a chair but chose to stand for much of the trial, resting against the dock and occasionally exchanging words with his legal team. The trial was unusually long in that it ran over two days, unlike most trials of the Victorian period which were completed within a day, with a jury's verdict being reached within a matter of minutes of completion of the judge's summing up. On the first day of the trial, 19 March, the proceedings lasted between 9am and 6.30pm. There had been some delay when eleven members of the jury had failed to answer to their names, resulting in fines of £5 being given to each of them.

On both days the evidence outlined here earlier was again repeated to the jurors.

That first day consisted of opening arguments and the prosecution's case presented by Mr Bliss. The jury was told that whilst the prosecution's case consisted of circumstantial evidence, there was sufficient proof that John was responsible and that the act of murder itself does not have to be witnessed in order for there to be certainty of a person's guilt. The dead man's skull was shown to the jury to demonstrate the ballistics evidence. John barely reacted when seeing it.

The defence case commenced on the second day of the trial and was led by Mr Sergeant Wilkins who argued that there was no evidence linking the defendant to his brother's death. A number of character references were also given with people who knew John testifying to his good character. He was described as a man possessing humanity, kindliness of disposition, steadiness, sobriety, amiability and general good conduct. Following a summing up of both prosecution and defence cases by the judge Mr Baron Platt, which lasted an hour and twenty minutes, the jury was asked to consider their verdict. The instruction was given at around 12.50am and after only eight minutes it was announced it had

---

CROWN COURT, WEDNESDAY, March 19.
Before Mr. Baron PLATT.
MURDER AT THURGOLAND.

The circumstance of a person being charged with the wilful murder of his brother, caused considerable interest to be manifested on the morning of the above day, to hear the trial, and at an early hour in the morning, the Court became crowded. The number of people in court caused two or three persons to faint, and they had to be carried out.

The learned JUDGE having taken his seat precisely at nine o'clock, the names of the jurors were called over, and eleven of those who did not answer were ordered to be fined £5 each. The jury having at length been sworn—

An extract from an article from the York Herald and General Advertiser *dated 22 March 1851 relating to the trial of John Firth for the murder of his brother George.*
(The author's collection)

reached their verdict. The foreman of the jury declared that they had unanimously found John Firth not guilty of the murder of George Firth.

Was John Firth wrongly acquitted? Was he lucky or a cunning killer with a good defence team who were able to fool a jury? Or was there truth in his story about the two men who had approached him and George in Dodworth? Was George therefore killed as a result of his drunken behaviour, which caused offence? Or did some other individual fire a fatal shot on that January night? The truth has been lost in history.

CHAPTER 2

The Shocking Death of the Bearded Lady (William Ratcliffe) (1883)

T he death of William Ratcliffe is as much a mystery today as it was in 1883, when he was found unconscious on the threshold of his Sheffield home on Sunday 7 October.

The scene of the deadly tale was 1 Court, Boden Lane, a small lane just of Rockingham Street close to Sheffield's city centre. The dwelling was referred to in the press at the time as a house

The only remaining 19th century buildings on Boden Lane, where William Ratcliffe lived and died. (The author)

in a 'miserable looking' and 'squalid' court. Much of Boden Lane was developed upon in recent times, although a small court and buildings dating to the nineteenth century can still be seen.

The 45-year-old victim of this story was known as 'the bearded lady' on account of his feminine appearance – apart from the beard – which included a small face and thin, long hands. He also spoke in an effeminate manner and occasionally dressed as a woman. In the past he had appeared at fairs as the bearded woman and sometimes read peoples' fortunes. In later life he had sold herbs and read fortunes in several of Sheffield's public houses. He had begun renting the dwelling at which he was found injured only five months before his death.

The hovel in which he was found, and his choice of lifestyle, was a far cry from his early adult life. William was a lifelong resident of Sheffield and had previously worked as a burnisher. His burial records state he was a 'scale-presser'. His father gave him £10 to better himself and for a time he was successful. He worked until he got married and at the time of his wedding he had £90 in savings; a significant sum for the times. Then his life changed. William became idle; and did not work. He squandered all of the money he had saved and so his marriage broke down and the couple separated. It was at this time that William began to cultivate the image of a woman. Ashamed of him, William's family refused to have anything to do with him and so William's life was destined to be one of poverty (he was described in newspaper articles as being 'wretchedly poor') and prejudice which would lead to his untimely death. He was buried in an unmarked grave in Section X at the City Road cemetery. With the letter 'X' often signifying the unknown or mysterious, it is perhaps apt that he was buried in that section of the cemetery.

William spent the night before his body was found the same way he spent most evenings. From the evidence of a number of witnesses we can build up what can only be assumed to be an accurate account of his movements, unless some of the evidence was misleading and provided by the attacker.

At around 6pm William was at his home when his friend Thomas Parkin, a table knife handle presser, arrived. At that time William 'was well, getting his tea' according to Parkin. When he finished the two men left and went to the end of Thomas Street to be shaved. Parkin left his companion at around 6.15pm and they agreed to meet at the Raven Hotel at the top end of Fitzwilliam Street – today the site of a modern restaurant and bars. William joined his friend at the hotel an hour later and they then began to walk around the town.

The pair were regulars at Wallace's vaults on Campo Lane and they paid a visit there that night. William often had no money but was usually given a free glass of ale by the landlord. On the Saturday night William visited Wallace's vaults and spoke briefly to the landlady before walking down into the bar. He seemed in good spirits and stayed in the bar for some time, drinking two glasses of beer paid for by Parkin. After finishing the drinks the

A late 19th century photograph of the junction of Campo Lane and Paradise Street, where William Ratcliffe drank hours before his death. (Photograph reproduced from the Picture Sheffield Collection, courtesy of Sheffield Local Studies Library)

two men went to the Paradise vaults nearby, where they drank more beer, leaving at around 9.30pm. They took a second walk and went through the market, before heading to the Pitcher and Glass or Virginia vaults on Paradise Street where they arrived at

Paradise Street from Paradise Square at some time between 1900 and 1919. It was on Paradise Street that William Ratcliffe drank hours before his death. (Photograph reproduced from the Picture Sheffield Collection, courtesy of Sheffield Local Studies Library)

10.15pm and left at 11pm. They then made their way home, with Parkin accompanying William most of the way towards Boden Lane, leaving him at St Thomas Street, Portobello, shortly after 11pm. It was assumed that William continued his walk home and did not deviate from it because, according to Parkin, William was afraid to walk alone after 11pm. Despite having had several glasses of ale, William was not so drunk that he was unable to walk. Indeed he could walk without assistance. Parkin had given William three and a half pence to buy more beer but William had not spent it. When he arrived home it was believed he began making supper between 12.15am and 12.30am.

Sometime after returning home, William was heard by neighbour Frederick Darwent to exclaim 'Oh poor Poll' but then nothing else was heard and Darwent thought nothing of it. Perhaps if he had, then this baffling case would make a little more sense. He thought it might have been a joke, because William enjoyed playing jokes on him. 'He has done so frequently in order to alarm me,' Darwent would later say. 'Only for fun and that has put me on my guard. Had he not done it before I should have run at once to him.'

At around 6am on the Sunday morning, Darwent left home for Askham's Works to clean out the engine and boiler. In the morning darkness he saw a cat in the yard. It was making a horrid noise which he later described as 'shrieking like a tiger'. He could also hear the sound of a person 'moaning', he would later claim. Darwent followed the cat and it ran to William's house. The door of the house was wide open and it took just moments to notice that William was laying face down on the ground across the threshold, in a pool of blood. His head was in the small channel leading from the kitchen slopstone. His head and arms were outside the house, but the rest of his body was inside the entrance. William was fully dressed except for a hat. He was unconscious but still alive, and was bleeding a little from both sides of his head. He had also vomited, no doubt from shock. Darwent went for help, attracting the attention of his neighbours. Some neighbours came to help and they managed to get William into his home and tried to make him as comfortable as possible, placing him on the floor next to his fireplace.

William Skinner, a surgeon from Broomhill described as the 'parish doctor', was sent for at request of the Union and arrived

at 8.15pm – fourteen hours after William was found. If medical
help had arrived earlier than perhaps the outcome may have
been different. Whilst he quickly realised there was little that could
be done to save William, he tried to give some treatment for
the injuries to reduce the suffering of the unfortunate man. These
injuries included bleeding from the nose and eye, although there
was no broken skin over the eye. There was a severe bruise over the
left eye but no other visible signs of violence.

Early press reports claimed William had two stab wounds to
both temples but these reports proved to be incorrect and were
probably based on the account of William bleeding from both sides
of his head, with a journalist jumping to conclusions. Inaccurate
reporting is a common problem and so great care has to be taken
when researching these old cases where newspaper archives form a
major source of information. Thankfully, inquests into deaths were
comprehensively covered in most cases and so accurate information relating to the circumstances of a death can be obtained from
coverage of inquest hearings. It was established that William's
injuries had been the result of a heavy blow to the head and it was
the doctor's opinion that it was very unlikely to have been inflicted
by accident.

Skinner visited again the following morning, shortly after 8am,
and found William to still be unconscious. Realising there was
nothing more that could be done the doctor left and at around
9.30am that same day William Ratcliffe died from his injuries.

When William's brother came to identify the body he said he had
not seen the deceased in several years and knew little about him.

An inquest into the death was held before the coroner Dossey
Wightman, at the George and Dragon Hotel on Broad Lane. The
inquest was adjourned after the coroner was given an outline by
the residents of the yard as to what they had, or had not, heard and
seen and to allow for further police investigations. It was concluded
on 19 October.

The medical evidence was discussed, with Mr Skinner testifying that the fatal blow to the head could not have been self
inflicted and must have been caused by some other individual. It
was his opinion that death was not the consequence of an accident.
'I have seen the place and I don't think the deceased could have
been injured to such an extent in that way [an accident] by any

THE SUPPOSED MURDER OF "THE BEARDED LADY."

THE ADJOURNED INQUEST.

The adjourned inquest on the body of William Ratcliffe, perhaps better known as the "bearded lady," who died on the 8th inst., under circumstances of the most suspicious character, was resumed yesterday afternoon at the George and Dragon Hotel, Broad lane, before Mr. Dossey Wightman.

An extract of an article from the Sheffield and Rotherham Independent *dated 20 October 1883 relating to the death of William Ratcliffe.* (The author's collection)

possibility,' he said. It was 'highly improbable' that he had simply fallen, the doctor added.

Death had been caused by bleeding to the brain, caused by the blow to the head, with the cranial cavity apparently having flooded with blood, and lots of clots were found during the post-mortem. There was an extensive fracture to the deceased's skull which extended from above the left eye, down the nose and to the base of the skull. William's stomach was in a very unhealthy state but this did not contribute to his death. After receiving the head injury it was Skinner's belief that William would not have been able to move and it would have been impossible to walk.

One of the other residents of the yard, George Richardson, did not see or hear William on the night of 6 October or morning of 7 October prior to the discovery of the injured man. He did not know anything untoward had occurred until Darwent called his attention at around 6am. He had gone to bed at around 11pm and heard nothing other than an acquaintance knocking on his door at some point following his retirement. The acquaintance, a man named William Henry Jones, wanted to stay there that night because he was too drunk to make his way home. Richardson allowed the visitor to stay, and Jones spent the night on the sofa. When Darwent called for Richardson it was Jones who answered the door and shouted upstairs to Richardson.

Richardson told the inquest that he never knew William to suffer any health problems, or have a tendency to fall, but did give an account of a curious statement made by him before he died. William had allegedly told Richardson that he was afraid of falling over when he had 'low feelings'. Richardson did not understand what was meant by this phrase.

Jones, a smith, did not hear or see anything of relevance. He knew the deceased by sight but had not seen him for between twelve and fourteen days. He did see the dying man when Darwent came to the house to raise the alarm.

Jones was regarded as a potential suspect. The coroner asked him directly why he had been so nervous and shaken on the morning that the body was discovered. Was this drunkenness or was he involved in the attack? Jones denied being responsible.

Jones did not have any visible blood upon his person or clothing when he arrived at Richardson's home, but that is not to say he was not involved because the injury may not have resulted in the transfer of blood on to the attacker. Nonetheless, there *was* some evidence to suggest Jones had no involvement in causing William's injury. Mrs Wragg, another neighbour of William's, said she saw Jones arrive at Richardson's home at around midnight. She had later gone into the yard at around 1am and had not seen William lying unconscious. She had remained awake for some unspecified but significant amount of time, with her door open, and neither saw nor heard anything. This would suggest the attack took place some time after 1am and unless Jones left the building during the early hours then he could not have been responsible. It is unlikely he would want to attack a man who he barely knew and in all probability he would have been in a heavy sleep due to the effects of his intoxication.

According to Parkin there had been no quarrel between him and William or between William and any other individual during the evening and night whilst they were drinking together. Parkin had no idea who could be responsible for an attack, if indeed there was an attack.

A member of the inquest jury offered what on the face of it seemed to be important information. He had been approached by a woman who claimed that William had told her just hours before he received his injury, that a man known locally as 'Pork Pie' had threatened to take his life. The deceased was apparently very afraid. If true then this could have been a significant lead.

If the case had gone to trial such evidence would have been regarded as hearsay evidence, which would not have been admissible, and scorn was certainly poured upon the story by the coroner and the police. The police had investigated the claim and

An unidentified Sheffield policeman from the late 19th century, possibly from around the time of the investigation into the death of William Ratcliffe. (Photograph reproduced from the Picture Sheffield Collection, courtesy of Sheffield Local Studies Library)

were able to confirm that the woman had seen the victim at around 11.15pm outside the Grapes Inn in Portobello. However, it was shown that 'Pork Pie' was in fact in the workhouse on the night of the attack and had been there since 2 July, leaving for only a few hours on 17 September. The coroner stated that he doubted most stories that he heard saying that 'they were not worth the wind that blew across them.'

A member of the jury stated that it was his belief that the police had had insufficient time to investigate the incident; a belief with which the coroner concurred. The police, however, disagreed. Sergeant McManus told the inquest that three officers had devoted a large amount of time and they were unable to investigate any further. This was on 19 October; less than two weeks after the attack.

The coroner's officer asked whether a reward could be offered for information but the coroner said this was not possible on account of there being insufficient evidence he was murdered.

As a consequence of the lack of evidence presented to the jury, they were only able to return the following verdict: 'That the deceased died on the 8th inst. from a fractured skull but as to how the injury was inflicted there is no evidence to show.'

The inquest jury only returned what we would today call an open narrative verdict because they did not have conclusive evidence to the contrary. The fact that rumour was discussed rather than fact did not help them in determining the truth. Yet the facts strongly suggest William was indeed the victim of a brutal murder. The medical evidence alone rules out an accident or suicide with almost medical certainty. The evidence of his neighbour who heard him exclaim 'Oh poor Polly' also suggests foul play because if he had fallen he would not have had time to utter these words before losing consciousness. Yet he would have had time if he knew he was going to be attacked and spoke the words immediately before being struck. That nobody heard another individual in the court is irrelevant because equally they did not hear William fall and heard nothing of him with the exception of Darwent who heard his exclamation.

Darwent found it strange that William's next-door neighbour did not try to help and did not hear the man moaning, or indeed anything relating to the incident. However, he attributed this to the couple being 'very elderly' and the wife having hearing problems.

Darwent was also surprised that he heard nothing but the exclamation which took place as he was going to bed. He did not hear any altercation but he could not rule out the possibility in his mind that foul play had occurred.

Earlier in the inquest Darwent gave his own theory. 'Well when it all comes to it, I think it will be found to have arisen from a grievance between Ratcliffe and some of his party,' but he had his doubts.

The position of the body is significant in understanding the circumstances which led to William's death. He was positioned as if he was coming out of his home and fell forward having been struck. He could not have tripped because there was nothing to trip over. If he had been going into his home then it would have been possible to have tripped forward over his step, but given he was facing in the opposite direction and more than half of his body was inside, he could not have tripped. Therefore, it would seem William answered the door to someone shortly after arriving home, unless he was in the habit of sleeping in his clothes, and was struck by someone who was stood just outside his house, causing him to

Section X of City Road Cemetery in Sheffield, where William Ratcliffe was buried in an unmarked grave. (The author)

fall to the ground in a forwardly direction. The medical man, upon visiting the scene, was, as has been said, certain it could not have been an accident.

Why then, did the police not believe the case was one of murder? Perhaps with the lack of definitive evidence that murder had been committed, it was easier for the police to believe that death had been a drunken accident. As a member of the lowest level of society, with stigma surrounding his choice of lifestyle and the lack of any family or friends who were able to put pressure on the authorities, there may have been a reluctance to investigate. Yet it seems certain that William was the victim of a murder which went unsolved because it was unrecognised for what it was.

As a Victorian transvestite could he have been the victim of a hate crime at a time when society was far less tolerant than at any time in living history? He was certainly subjected to a large amount of scorn and verbal abuse on account of his appearance and lifestyle. Perhaps someone took their prejudices too far ... with murderous consequences.

CHAPTER 3

Death of a Draper: The Mysterious Case of Florence Hargreaves (1926)

It was Wednesday, 27 January 1926, and the lead story in the *Yorkshire Telegraph and Star* was a 'Farmer's Divorce Court Story of "Love" in a Cottage.' Other stories that day included a former Worcester police officer who was sentenced to death for committing three murders in order to gain £70, an Anglo Italian debt agreement signed in London, and two steam ships drifting at the mercy of severe gales and 'mountainous seas' in the mid-Atlantic. That day was also to see an event closer to the homes of that newspaper's readership and which was to dominate the news for the next few weeks.

The story involved a woman named Florence Hargreaves who was an eccentric character well known in the Attercliffe area of Sheffield. She chose to speak to few, and most of those she did speak to felt the 54-year-old spinster was very terse towards them. She lived shut away from the outside world, yet ironically her death would be so mysterious, as mysterious as the woman herself, that people across Yorkshire and even other parts of the country followed events with immense fascination and discussed the case at length speculating upon how this woman lost her life.

Whilst people were reading about love in a cottage a crowd began to form outside a drapery shop at 697 Attercliffe Road. It was a very small shop, consisting of just one small room, with a small amount of space above the shop which was used to form a home. Amongst the wares in the shop were what was originally described as 'a modern collection of children's garments, blouses, ribbons, cottons and silks.' It would later be described in more

A photograph of Florence Hargreaves. (The author's collection)

detail, with the window display being described as having clothing 'jumbled up in the bottom without any semblance of order' and with coats and skirts blocking the view through the remaining part of the window. The shop was very dirty, both inside and out, so much so that the text on the sign above the door was barely visible.

There Florence Hargreaves had lived and worked, running the shop for around twenty years, but there had been growing concern about her as January began to come to a close. These concerns culminated on that Wednesday afternoon.

Florence had not opened the premises on Saturday but this was not at first believed to be suspicious because she had been

Attercliffe Road at around the time that Florence Hargreaves began working in her shop. Her shop can just be seen towards the right of the photograph. (Photograph reproduced from the Picture Sheffield Collection, courtesy of Sheffield Local Studies Library)

'negligent' according to neighbours and sometimes did not open the shop. She also occasionally left things outside her shop at night and did not seem to think that they could be stolen. She led a rather secluded life and would occasionally not be seen for two or three days at a time. Those who owned shops nearby told journalists that they hardly knew the woman. One who had been a neighbour for 20 years, since Florence moved to the area, said only a few words had been exchanged in all of that time. She 'kept herself to herself" neighbours would later say. She was short and sharp towards her customers and people wondered how she managed to make a living. Her stock was very old and out of fashion, it was claimed, and it was speculated some of it had been there for as long as Florence had occupied the shop.

One customer told a journalist about her own experiences and knowledge of the deceased: 'If you went into her shop and did not buy the article which she showed you, she would take it out of your hand and fling it carelessly on a shelf and walk away as if she was vexed. It was this peculiarity no doubt which accounted for her declining clientele, and business of late had been very bad with her. She was a very emotional type of woman. One moment she would be in the best of spirits, and the next would find her in the depths of despair.'

Mrs Kent, a fellow draper from Wincobank who worked with her mother and had known Florence for 13 or 15 years, told a journalist that the dead woman 'had neither enemies nor friends. She treated everyone alike – very indifferently.'

Kent did, however, describe some redeeming features of the woman: 'She was often standing at the door and as I knew her in business she never failed to say "Good morning". I have often stopped to chat with her and she used to say she was not doing very well. She certainly did very little business lately. We found her rather a peculiar woman but she was always very amiable to us. From what I have heard from her customers she was very funny to them but when I wanted anything for a customer she would always supply it to me at cost and was always very friendly. She never came to see us, but although when I left Newhall Road I invited her to do so and she said she would.'

Florence would rarely buy produce, including what the press referred to as 'the necessities of life', from neighbouring shops, choosing instead to travel long distances to buy these items.

The police were contacted when by Wednesday 27 January Florence had still not been seen and her shop remained closed. Knowing that she had family in Rawmarsh the police began making some enquiries in that area. Neighbours had made the assumption she was in Rawmarsh where she visited at weekends and the police thought this was possibly the case.

The police contacted Florence's 80-year-old father James Hargreaves, who lived at Green Lane, Rawmarsh, and worked as a boot maker, but he told officers that he had not seen his daughter. She had said she would visit, but did not. Accompanied by Florence's sister, Mary Brameld, James had travelled to Attercliffe to check on his daughter.

When the pair arrived at the shop on that January afternoon they found it locked. They called to Florence, trying to attract her attention, but received no response. With their concerns at tremendous levels they sought the assistance of a locksmith, H. H. Constantine, whose shop was a few doors down. They feared that Florence might be unwell or had had an accident. They needed to gain access to the shop to check on her, and with the front door locked and the rear door fastened with a chain, seeking Constantine's help seemed the only possible course of action.

The entry was attended by Superintendent Hughes, the Chief of Attercliffe Division. When they managed to open the door and gain entry it did not take long to establish that perhaps even their worst fears had been surpassed by the reality.

Florence was found lying face down behind the shop counter. Her body was fully clothed with heavy layers of clothing, gaiters such as those worn outdoors, and stout laced boots. According to Police Constable Ernest Sharpe who was present during the discovery of the body, Florence was 'lying face downwards with some clothing over her head and her skirt in a disordered condition.' Although her clothing was slightly disarranged, it would later be confirmed there was no suspicion of sexual assault. A cotton stocking was tied tightly round her neck, with the knot tied at the back of her neck. She had blood on both of her hands and there was hair entangled between the fingers on one of her hands. There was an apron beneath her head which was saturated with blood.

After viewing the body Constable Sharpe ran to a nearby shop in order to telephone the local police station to request assistance.

When Inspector Joseph Wainwright examined the scene he found no visible evidence for a struggle between Florence and any other individual. He also found the back door fastened with a chain. It is unclear whether it was fully secure or merely closed with a chain in place, which could perhaps have been fastened from the outside. The key to the front door was at first believed to be missing because it could not be found. However, days after the discovery of the body the key was found in the front part of the premises.

Before the police arrived a crowd had already begun to form outside the shop and it continued to grow. It remained outside the shop for several hours for every day of the investigation whilst the police remained on the premises, with the members of the crowd not being deterred even by cold drizzle. The bystanders began to speculate about what might have happened and it was not long before the whole community was discussing a terrible poisoning which had cost the draper her life. The shop was inspected by Deputy Chief Constable G. H. Barker, Chief Superintendent Hollis, Superintendent Hughes, several other officers and the police surgeon, Dr Geoffrey Carter, who certified death and was to later perform the post-mortem. He inspected the scene as well as attending to the corpse, in order to gain a full understanding of how Florence could have lost her life.

There was no evidence at the scene to immediately show the full circumstances of what could have caused Florence's death. What was described as a thorough search of the scene was undertaken, with the premises being searched from roof to cellar. No weapons were found or any other clues which were believed to be directly involved in the tragedy.

There was nothing obviously missing and the police concluded that nothing had been stolen. However, just because nothing appeared to have been stolen does not mean that nothing was taken, plus the annals of criminal history are filled with examples

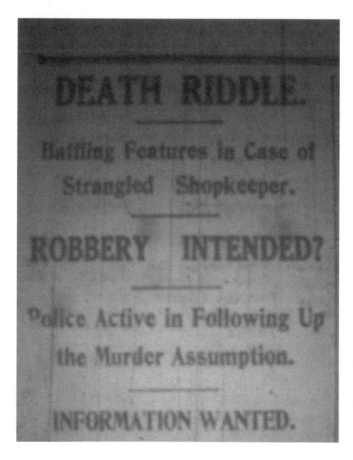

An extract of an article relating to the death of Florence Hargreaves.
(The author's collection)

of murders which have been undertaken by someone intending to commit burglary or robbery, who has then fled empty handed out of panic or because they discovered there was nothing worth stealing but by which time they had already taken a life. In fact, the evidence suggests that something may well have been stolen. Inspector Wainwright found an empty leather moneybag neatly folded in the shop and the only money in the shop was a postal order worth five shillings. Although times were undoubtedly very tough for Florence, were they so tough that she had not a penny in cash?

Florence had been robbed approximately a year earlier. A burglar had managed to gain access to her shop through removing roof tiles. The draper had fled the shop in fear. She had been very lackadaisical with regards to security and her own personal safety, but that frightening experience had caused her to assess her habits and according to neighbours security had been stepped up. The shop was no longer left unlocked at night or when she went out, though she was still negligent at times. Could someone have returned expecting there to be something worth stealing?

In the days after the discovery of Florence's death it was revealed that there had been a series of petty thefts in shops on Attercliffe Road and elsewhere in Attercliffe Common. Could it be possible that Florence's shop was targeted?

Prior to Florence's father stepping foot in the shop a bailiff walked in, as Florence owed money for her rates. He had come to issue a distress warrant but was asked by the police to leave because an investigation was in progress. He left the warrant in the shop. This would imply that Florence was in grave financial problems but still it would be expected she would have a small amount of money. Her financial problems may not have been known by a burglar, if indeed she was robbed. Alternatively of course, she may have wanted to commit suicide as a desperate measure to escape her problems and this was the favoured opinion of the police during the early stages of the investigation. Newspaper reports stated that her shop would have to be sold to pay for her debts.

Florence often visited the Washford Road Railway Bridge for some unknown reason, returning a few minutes later in an 'irritable mood' according to newspaper reports. Otherwise there was no evidence of any depression or suicidal thoughts.

Washford Bridge in Attercliffe Sheffield in 1929. It was here that Florence Hargreaves occasionally visited, returning afterwards in an irritable mood. (Photograph reproduced from the Picture Sheffield Collection, courtesy of Sheffield Local Studies Library)

There were no evident signs of violence, the police told journalists, but this information was very wrong. There was no evidence of any disorder in the shop but the evidence of violence was clear from the injuries on the dead woman's body.

Almost from the outset, before other possibilities had been investigated, the police had become convinced that Florence had committed suicide. 'Tragic Death of Woman Draper: Theory of Suicide' was the headline in the *Yorkshire Telegraph and Star* on the day after Florence's body was found.

One officer was quoted as saying 'All will depend on what the post-mortem tells us' but the police had seemingly made up their mind despite their initial reticence to make public statements. That post-mortem took place on the 28 January and was to raise serious questions about the initial police assumption. It also suggested the very real possibility that Florence Hargreaves had died in a very brutal murder.

The inquest opened on the Friday 29 January before the coroner, Mr J. Kenyon Parker. A preliminary examination of the case was undertaken in order to give the coroner and inquest jury an outline of the evidence from the witnesses who discovered the body, and also the medical evidence, with the post-mortem having now been completed.

James Hargreaves gave evidence of his daughter's health. She was in good health when he last saw her, he told the inquest. He had been expecting Florence to visit him on the Sunday at his home in Rawmarsh but she never arrived. He had found this unusual and his concern was increased when he discovered on the following Wednesday that his daughter had not been seen. He said that she had her 'ups and downs' like most people do, but that as far ashe was

J Kenyon Parker, the coroner who presided over the inquest into the death of Florence Hargreaves. (The author's collection)

concerned she was not depressed or suicidal. He described going to the shop and upon entry seeing his daughter's body.

When asked if there should have been any money in the shop which may have been stolen, James told the coroner, 'Well, it is quite likely she had, but I had no means of knowing what it was or where it was.'

Dr Carter presented an overview of the findings of his post-mortem which certainly showed the poisoning theory was nothing more than idle gossip. He said that in addition to the stocking which had caused strangulation, the victim had two severe wounds to her scalp, fractured ribs and extensive bruising.

Going into detail about the injuries, the doctor stated that the dead woman's hands had been moved before he was able to examine the body. Nonetheless, he was able to see they were both blood-stained and he saw the hair between the fingers. The right hand was also badly swollen and discoloured, with a layer of diffused blood at the back of the hand. None of the bones in the hands were fractured. There was blood on the outer items of clothing that Florence was wearing. Her face showed signs of livid which, although not discussed in the coverage of the inquest, proved that she had been face down immediately after her death long enough for the blood to settle around her face. Her tongue was livid and protruding and her lips were swollen and bruised. Her right eye was badly swollen and her right eyelid bruised. There was also a bruise on the middle of the forehead. There was haemorrhage on the surface of her left eye. From the left eye upwards Florence's forehead was swollen and just above the left eye there was a deep discolouration. There were no signs of fracture to the skull.

On the left hand side of the scalp, on the dome of the skull, there was a jagged wound so deep that the skull was visible, although the bone itself was not damaged. A portion of the scalp had been torn away when this injury was caused. There was a second vertical laceration at the back of Florence's head, slightly to the right hand side, three quarters of an inch in length which penetrated as far as the skull.

There was a wound all of the way round Florence's neck, with hardened and discoloured skin, and the windpipe showed signs of compression. This was caused by the stocking which acted as a very tight ligature and caused Florence's death through strangulation. The knot had been tied at the back of Florence's neck, slightly to the left of the spine.

Six of Florence's ribs had been fractured; the second, third, fourth, fifth, sixth and seventh ribs on the right hand side of her body. There was also blood outside of the ribs. There was also bruising to both forearms, which the doctor believed may have been caused by a thumb (or both thumbs) being pressed hard against the skin.

The contents of Florence's stomach showed she had eaten tripe one or two hours before her death. Other than some slight kidney degeneration her internal organs were in a relatively healthy state. Although her clothing had been slightly disturbed, there was no evidence of any 'interference', the doctor stated.

Summing up the results of his post-mortem examination Dr Carter told the inquest: 'I came to the following conclusions. First that death had probably taken place some three days prior to my examination. Secondly that food had been taken around two hours before death. And thirdly that the immediate cause of death was strangulation preceded by injuries to the head and chest.'

The coroner put a question to him to which everyone was interested to know the answer. 'Taking that strangulation alone Dr Carter, do you think that could be accidental?' 'No sir', Dr Carter replied, adding that if only the strangulation was to be considered it could possibly have been suicide. However, there were of course the other injuries to consider. With reference to these injuries he told the inquest, 'They could not all have been produced accidentally.'

Dr Carter continued, saying that he had concerns about the belief Florence had committed suicide. 'I am suspicious. In regard to my statement that the injuries may not all have been produced accidentally I mean the injuries could have been produced in a street accident, but not accidentally in the house.'

The intimation was clear; Florence had not, in his medical opinion, committed suicide but had been beaten violently before being strangled to death. This was the suggestion he raised to the coroner and it was this belief which needed to be investigated.

Barker, Hollis and Hughes were all present at the inquest and they requested that the case be adjourned to allow them to undertake further inquiries into the matter.

The coroner agreed to adjourn the inquest until 11 February and expressed his hope that all of the interest in the local community

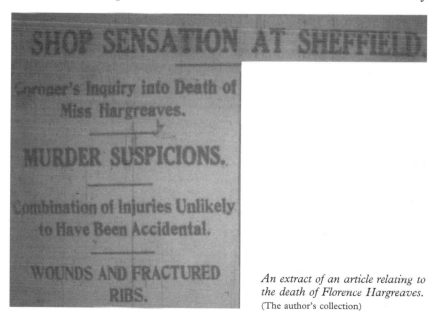

An extract of an article relating to the death of Florence Hargreaves.
(The author's collection)

and in the newspapers would result in any useful information being brought to the police's attention.

Although she was generally disliked in the community where she ran her shop, in Rawmarsh from where she had originated, Florence was respected, perhaps because the community respected the family as a whole. On the afternoon of 30 January Florence was buried at the Haigh Road cemetery in Rawmarsh, and the route of the funeral cortège was lined with mourners. Large floral tributes were given for the dead woman. The grave is shared with Florence's step-mother Mary and the inscription on the headstone reads, 'Mary the beloved wife of James Hargreaves died 11 July 1917 age 75 years. Also, Florence Hargreaves his beloved daughter who was suddenly called home January 22nd 1926 – age 54 years.'

When the inquest resumed on 11 February, Superintendent Hollis requested a further adjournment. He told the coroner that the police inquiries had changed focus on the basis of the medical evidence. Whilst they had originally been convinced the case was one of suicide, prior to any medical examination being performed, they were now erring towards the belief that Florence had died at the hands of another person who thus far was unidentified. He told the coroner that whilst the evidence so far did not prove anything either way, it 'pointed rather strongly to actual murder'. The coroner expressed his desire to assist the police, but seemed to only reluctantly allow another adjournment, with the inquest resuming on 25 February. At this time, those sitting on a jury at an inquest were typically middle class business owners and were not reimbursed for having their businesses closed whilst performing their civic duty. As a result it was not unknown for inquests to be hurried along.

A £50 reward for information identifying who was responsible for causing Florence's death was offered, but it went unclaimed.

It was important for the detectives to establish Florence's movements in the days before her body was discovered in order to determine when she may have died.

Mrs C. Ford, who worked in a sweet shop and newsagents close to Florence's shop, said that the dead woman had visited her shop on the Thursday 21 January to get a paper. 'She appeared to be interested in Rotherham news always. She was a very eccentric woman,' Ford recalled. This shop was presumably the one owned by Mr E. H. Harvey who described her as being 'in her usual

A Sheffield Police Constable wearing the winter police uniform. The photograph dates to 1928 but would be the same or similar to that worn by officers investigating the death of Florence Hargreaves. (Photograph reproduced from the Picture Sheffield Collection, courtesy of Sheffield Local Studies Library)

health' when she bought a newspaper from his shop on that Thursday. She returned the following day at 11.15am to buy a sports newspaper but he had sold out of copies.

The police were anxious to trace a boy who called at Florence's shop on the Saturday morning before her body was discovered. He visited in order to take a message, in the form of a note, to Florence but was unable to deliver it because the shop was locked and he received no answer to his knocking. Was Florence dead by this time? After knocking for some time he went to the shop next door and asked the shop worker if 'Mrs Atkinson' was in. It was established that the boy was after Florence Hargreaves and his mistake regarding the name was on account of the block of shops and other properties to which Florence's shop belonged, had once been owned by a man named Richard Atkinson. Florence had once worked for Atkinson and his name still appeared above the door of the shop, although it was obscured by a thick layer of dirt, and the boy must therefore have assumed that Florence was Atkinson's wife. Despite appeals for the boy to come forward he was never identified and the contents of the message he wanted to deliver that morning were never ascertained. It seems unlikely that the note would have related to financial matters because if it had, it would have been addressed to Florence Hargreaves and not Mrs Atkinson.

A man who had known Florence for a number of years claimed he had seen the dead woman on Saturday evening. On 2 February he gave a statement to the police at the station on Whitworth Lane to the effect that he saw Florence as he was boarding a tram. He saw her cross over from Newhall Road and at one point there was little distance between them. He was certain of his identification despite doubts from the police. 'She was carrying a parcel which looked like food,' he claimed. It was his impression that the parcel may have been a portion of fish and chips.

The police doubted the man's story on account that there were chip shops closer to her shop than where Florence had been seen. However, it has already been said that Florence was known to travel further than necessary for 'the necessities of life'. Perhaps she walked to a chip shop at a greater distance than those close to her shop in the same way that she walked further than necessary to buy her groceries and other produce. Detectives did visit each of the chip shops in the area, however, to speak to the owners and establish whether Florence may have visited that evening. It was assumed that if Florence had visited a chip shop it would have been the one at 235 Newhall Road, which was the closest, but the owner, George Butler had no recollection of seeing her at all. The police therefore dismissed the man's story of seeing Florence which may have been a mistake for the reason stated above but also because there was no conclusive evidence the package was fish and chips. It could have been any food product, perhaps the tripe which Florence was known to have eaten shortly before she died. By ruling out the sighting on potentially flawed reasoning, the police may have made a major error in their understanding of the case.

A sinister looking man had called at the shop next door to Florence's shop on the Friday evening, it was claimed. The man had been dressed in women's clothing and had a bloodstained hand. The shopkeeper, Mrs Askin, had been so terrified that she sold the man cigarettes, breaking the law in doing so. This story was also doubted, with the police claiming it was probably 'all fiction'.

Another fictional story was that a well-known local thief had offered his services to the police to help identify, through the criminal fraternity, who had killed Florence. 'I have never heard of such a thing,' Hollis told the press when dismissing the story. 'People who circulate such stories are not at all helpful in a very serious and difficult task,' another officer said.

The police had believed that Florence had died on the Friday which was consistent with the claim of the sinister man. It was not until the witness came forward claiming to have seen Florence the following evening that they considered revising their view. With that sighting dismissed, if indeed it was incorrect, then the evidence continues to point towards death taking place on the Friday night. Dr Carter's opinion was that Florence had been dead for three days by the time her body was found on the Wednesday afternoon, but he accepted that death could have taken place earlier.

Certainly on Saturday morning the boy with the note received no response to his knocking on the door. And Florence failed to keep to her usual activities that day. Every Saturday morning for several years she had visited the newsagents of Mr E. H. Harvey at 264 Newhall Road in order to buy the newspapers, but on the Saturday morning she never visited. The reason for her regular visits to the shop was because she was passionate about football and liked to keep fully informed of the match results. According to Mr Harvey she would have visited on the Saturday if she was alive and well. It was also his belief that the draper would fight any attacker and there would therefore be signs of a struggle, but that assumes she saw her attacker (if there was one) and had time to embark in a fight for her life. She may quite easily have been quickly overcome.

When the inquest resumed on 25 February the 'dark mystery', as the *Yorkshire Telegraph and Star* called it, was still unresolved. The police were represented by Superintendent Hollis, Superintendent Hughes and Inspector Naylor who were of the opinion a murder had been committed. The coroner told the jury that he had received a part of the police paperwork relating to the case and had gone through 34 foolscap sheets of paper but still could not be sure what had taken place.

The medical evidence was repeated to the jury by Dr Carter and this time he gave additional information about how the injuries may have been caused. The two head wounds were approximately five inches apart and this corresponded exactly with the distance between the spikes on an iron gate within the shop, he said. One of the spikes had been bent and there was blood on the gate as well as bloodstains on various parts of the shop including a table cloth and on a wall. It seemed certain, therefore, that Florence had injured her head on the gate but how this happened remained a mystery. The spikes were 4ft 11in off the ground and Florence was only 5ft 4in in height. It was felt she must have stumbled backwards or been pushed on to the spikes.

Another curious aspect to the case was that Florence was wearing her coat, under which were the long ends of the stocking, running down her back. As such, the stockings had been tied round her neck before her coat had been put on. If she intended to commit suicide why would she wish to put a coat on, knowing that her death was imminent? Equally why if someone had strangled her to death would they then place a coat on the victim? It is possible that Florence had tied the stocking around her neck herself to act as a scarf because of the cold weather. She would not have tied the stocking tightly enough to kill herself by accident, of course, but any assailant who desired to kill the shopkeeper may have tightened the stocking, rendering her dead after violently beating her.

The doctor reiterated his medical opinion that cause of death was strangulation. When asked whether the injuries could have occurred accidentally or intentionally by Florence and then the deceased strangled herself, Dr Carter said this was impossible. He explained that Florence's right hand was so badly maimed that she would not have been able to tie the stocking around her neck so tightly. When asked if it was possible the injuries could have occurred after the knot was tied, the doctor again said this was impossible. 'In my opinion they could not all have been caused by a fall, which would have ensued within thirty seconds. The wounds on the head might well have been caused by a fall backwards on the spikes,' he said. Even if the head wounds were caused by a fall backwards, this did not account for the broken ribs, bruising to the forearms or injuries to the face. It also did not explain how Florence's body was away from the gate when found.

The coroner seemed unwilling to accept that the medical evidence ruled out suicide and also ruled out the possibility of accidental death. He said: 'It seems to me that there is very grave suspicion but no definite proof. The evidence which points to murder is almost entirely the evidence of the medical man and his examinations and tests. There is no evidence of any struggle or any interference with the deceased woman. What theory the police have I do not know and it is not a matter of importance that either you or I should know, because you form your verdict solely on the evidence. The case would be absolutely different if the police should put before them evidence which pointed to a particular person or persons being suspected of the crime.'

He added that the police had made very extensive enquiries and had found no evidence which pointed certainly towards Florence having died as a result of a murderous attack upon her. He said that therefore the jury, in his opinion, could not be in a position to express a firm verdict of wilful murder against a person or persons unknown. He did not believe there was anything other than a very small practical benefit in returning such a verdict in this case, which is a very curious thing to say. The practical benefit of such a verdict is to recognise a murder for exactly what it is. The only possible verdict they could return, he told the jury, was an open verdict and he told the jury quite clearly that this is what he would be inclined to advise them to do.

The coroner's opinion evidently swayed the jury sufficiently to return an open verdict, which recorded that Florence Hargreaves died through strangulation but the circumstances by which she came to be strangled were unknown. However, there was ample evidence to justify a murder verdict. In my opinion there is no doubt that Florence Hargreaves was the victim of a horrific murder, a murder which went unrecognised and as a consequence went unsolved.

It should be remembered that coroners during the early twentieth century were not medical professionals. They had no medical training. They were also not detectives. Whilst the police did not originally believe the case to be one of murder they did accept that Florence was almost certainly murdered when the case was investigated more thoroughly. Their suspicions were based upon the medical evidence and whilst there was no evidence proving the guilt of an individual or individuals, that does not mean that Florence was not killed. If every unsolved murder was given an open verdict due to the lack of evidence proving the guilt of the guilty party it would result in far fewer murders being recorded. It is of significance that both the police and the medical expert believed that Florence was the victim of foul play.

It was not surprising that Dr Carter's expert opinion was one of murder. It has been said, but must be stressed, that the medical evidence proved that Florence could not have strangled herself after receiving the other injuries. Her severely maimed hand would have made it impossible to tie the knot around her neck so tightly. Such a task would have required both hands yet only one was capable of sufficient strength. Equally she could not have inflicted the other injuries upon her person, either deliberately or through accident, after strangling herself because there would have been insufficient time to cause the several injuries and besides there were no objects in the shop which could have been responsible for causing every one of the injuries. Not all of them could have been caused by a fall. Therefore suicide and accident have to be eliminated.

Florence was struck repeatedly in the face and chest by someone using a blunt instrument which caused her ribs to break and the injuries on her face. She must have then fallen or been pushed on to the gate, perhaps during a struggle, piercing the back of her head with spikes from the gate. The fact she was conscious when she sustained the head injuries is evident from the fact one of her hands was covered in blood and hairs were entangled between her fingers. Clearly she had put her hand on her head to stem the flow of blood.

Bruises on her forearms were caused by a thumb (or both thumbs) being pressed hard against the skin, suggesting she had been grabbed at around the time of her death.

She had tried to defend herself from her attacker, thus proving there was a struggle contrary to what the police claimed. Her hand was severely maimed, being swollen and with major bruising and blood clotting at the back of it. This could only have been caused by a heavy blunt instrument striking her hand if she had raised it to protect herself. Perhaps she raised her hand to shield her face and the back of the hand was struck. After being struck violently, the killer tightened the stocking around her neck and left her to die. The disturbance of Florence's clothing, albeit slight though noticeable enough to remark upon, further suggests either a struggle or that Florence's body was moved or touched after death.

How then could the coroner have said there was no definite evidence of murder? There can be no doubt when considering the above that Florence was violently attacked. There does not have to be a disordered crime scene to prove that a struggle took place. The struggle could have been so quickly executed that little or nothing got disturbed, or the killer could well have tidied up after committing the murder, something which criminal history has shown to be a very common practice.

The absence of money in the shop could suggest Florence was robbed and killed, but by whom? The police did not have any suspects but that is not to say no one was responsible. With an open verdict returned at the inquest, in spite of the evidence pointing firmly towards murder, the culprit was unlikely to be caught because the police investigation had to end unless significant new evidence came to light. Police resources would be used for other crimes. It is unfortunate that a flawed opinion of a coroner effectively dictated to the police whether a crime should be regarded as a crime.

What about the sinister man dressed as a woman with the bloodstained hand who visited the shop next door on the Friday before Florence's body was discovered? If indeed Florence died on the Friday then is it not possible the sighting was correct? If Florence was murdered her killer would have been covered in blood. It is not unreasonable to suggest that he would have needed to change clothing in order to flee, and with an abundance of women's clothing available in the shop he changed into some and hoped that the blood on his hand would not be seen. The story may have been a fabrication, and it certainly was not believed, but unlike the other pieces of gossip which circulated after Florence's death, the tale of the man dressed as a woman came direct from the person who ran the shop and not from someone who had heard a story through Chinese whispers.

Whilst it is difficult to conceive that a murderer could have entered and left the shop which was locked, it has already been shown that accident and suicide can be eliminated as possible hypotheses. Yet this apparent locked room mystery is not so difficult to comprehend. It has already been suggested that the killer could have secured a chain from the outside of the shop after leaving the shop. The door was not actually bolted or locked in any other way. It may have taken time to put a chain in place from the outside but it can be done.

However, there is another possibility. It has been said that Florence's shop had once been burgled by a criminal entering through the roof. Whilst there were no roof tiles missing, or at least the police did not notice roof tiles having been removed when they inspected the building days after Florence was killed, the possibility that someone used the roof as a means of entry should not be ignored. Until recent decades, terraced buildings, such as that in which Florence lived and worked, had a loft space which had no barriers between properties. Anyone who lived in, or had access to, the terrace could easily have managed to get into Florence's shop. Even if roof tiles had not been removed from above Florence's drapery shop a criminal could have entered from above another shop. They could have left using the same means, or through the back door before chaining that door, as has been discussed. It is a fact that someone had entered Florence's shop from the roof on one occasion in the past. It is therefore not inconceivable that someone may have entered the shop using the same, or a similar method on a second occasion.

As the great fictional detective Sherlock Holmes often said: 'If you eliminate the impossible whatever remains, no matter how improbable, must be the truth.' Florence Hargreaves did not commit suicide. She did not die as the result of an accident. She was, therefore, murdered and her murder remains unsolved.

CHAPTER 4

The Murder of a Barnsley Gangster: The Death of Mark Scott (1931)

n Monday, 17 August 1931, the Hillsborough Park Cinema began showing a production called 'Murder Will Out'. 'Can you solve the mystery?' is what potential cinemagoers were asked in adverts in the *Yorkshire Telegraph and Star* (which was to be renamed *The Star* seven years later) and on billboards. Three days later the cinema showed another murder mystery, 'Under Suspicion'. Little would people in South Yorkshire have realised that so soon after these films were shown, there would be a real life murder mystery in the small mining town of Barnsley. Certainly, in this case someone would be under suspicion, but ultimately the culprit of this foul deed would remain at liberty and his identity would remain a mystery.

In fact, two deaths took place within the space of little more than a week, though only one would be regarded as murder.

Charles Smith, who was aged 72 or 73, was found unconscious on the floor at his home in Keresforth Road in Barnsley. A man named George Thompson, 53, was seen emerging from the house. Investigation of the scene revealed Smith had suffered a fractured skull and that death was due to a brain haemorrhage. It transpired he was struck, fell and cracked his head.

On 26 August Thompson was charged with the murder. He denied wilful murder, claiming that he pushed Smith away in self defence when the elderly man moved to strike him. After two adjournments to the proceedings, during which time Thompson had been granted bail, all charges against him were dropped on 17 September 1931.

Hillsboro' Park Cinema.

TWICE NIGHTLY: 6.30 & 8.40.

MONDAY, AUGUST 17th, 1931:

"MURDER WILL OUT,"

FEATURING:

Jack Mulhall, Lila Lee, Noah Beery & Tully Marshall.

CAN YOU SOLVE THE MYSTERY?

You'll miss a lot of guesses but get a lot of thrills.

THURSDAY, AUGUST 20th, 1931:

"UNDER SUSPICION,"

FEATURING:

Lois Moran & J. Harold Murray.

The Best Film these two Artists have acted in.

DON'T MISS THIS PICTURE!

THE ACOUSTIC PROPERTIES OF OUR CINEMA ARE ACKNOWLEDGED TO BE THE BEST IN THE DISTRICT.

WATCH THE......

HILLSBORO' PARK CINEMA

FOR THE BEST FILMS.

Come Next Week and See for Yourselves.

An advertisement for plays which appeared in Yorkshire newspapers in August 1931. (The author's collection)

The coroner presiding over the case, Mr C. J. Howarth, told those present: 'A charge has been made against a man, but the magistrates have arrived at the conclusion that there is no case to send the man for trial. I have had an opportunity of considering all the details and I don't think that there is any further evidence I can put before you. The matter will not be proceeded with further.'

Whether Thompson was lucky and provided a false story which was believed by the magistrates, or he was telling the truth and he killed in self defence, is uncertain but the outcome was that Smith's death was no longer considered to be a case of murder.

What *was* certainly a case of murder took place just days after charges were brought against Thompson. Yet this too would result in an accused man being released without charge before any trial took place

It was a time of change in Britain. Following the Wall Street Crash in 1929 a great depression spread across large parts of the western world. In Britain the economic crisis led to a major imbalance in the budget and a run on the pound. This resulted in decreased confidence in the Labour government of the day. Splits in the cabinet compounded the problems and on 24 August 1931 the government resigned. That same day, after discussions with King George V and the leaders of the Conservative and Liberal parties, Ramsey MacDonald agreed to form a National Government until a general election was held. It was in this time of economic uncertainty that the following foul deed took place.

At 6.20am on Wednesday, 26 August 1931, as he made his way to work, a boy named Wilfred Featherstone was startled to see a man staggering in the street, clearly seriously wounded. He was half doubled over as he moved and was clutching his stomach. The man was trying to make his way across Shambles Street from Graham's Orchard towards Windmill Yard, in the town centre. Much of this area has been developed upon in recent decades, with very little of the character as it had appeared during the 1930s surviving.

When asked by Featherstone what was wrong the man replied that he had been stabbed. He was bleeding very heavily and was clearly in a state of shock. He managed to make his way to a large stone at the bottom of Windmill Yard where he slumped, in what was described as a state of collapse. It was noticed that both his hands were covered with dried blood. Concerned, Featherstone

Shambles Street, Barnsley, where Mark Scott was fatally wounded. (The author)

went to seek help and he soon met Police Constable Barraclough on Shambles Street. The officer looked at the man's injuries and noted a severe wound, approximately four inches long, on the left-hand side of his abdomen, and a second injury on his left thigh. Barraclough telephoned for the police ambulance and the injured man was taken to the Beckett Hospital.

It was quickly established that the man was unemployed Mark Scott, 33, who had previously worked as a miner for several years. He had had to give up work a few months before the attack due to nystagmus, a condition causing involuntary eye movement which can result in limited vision. Mark was a keen football supporter and had lived at 39 Albert Street in Barnsley with his wife or partner, Mary Elizabeth Smith for 14 years. (He was said to be a married man but accounts conflicted and so I will refer to her simply as Mary Smith. Mark certainly lived with a woman who had been previously married to another man. Mary had one child, aged 14, from that previous marriage. She had six children in all, and it appears from their ages – nine months to ten years – that Mark was the father to five of them.) With only one child of working age in the household there were concerns that the family would find themselves in increasing hardship.

On arrival at hospital Mark was still alive and conscious but was in a state of shock. At no point in time did he give any indication as to who had attacked him. He gave no information of relevance at all despite questions being asked of him. Mary Smith visited him in hospital at around 8am, having been taken to the hospital by the police, and although Mark recognised her he did not tell his partner how he came to be injured.

Dr David Fitzpatrick, the resident surgical officer at the hospital, operated in an attempt to save Mark's life, but he died as a result of his injury later in the afternoon, at around 4.10pm. Shock and general peritonitis following puncture of the intestines was the surgeon's belief as to the cause of death. A post-mortem carried out by Dr P. L. Sutherland, a pathologist employed by the county council, confirmed the cause of death. The laceration to the abdominal wall was three inches in length. The wound to the thigh was two inches in length and quarter of an inch deep. The injuries had been caused by a sharp knife

It was believed that the fatal knife wounds had been inflicted several hours before Mark was seen, perhaps as many as eight hours previously, and most probably on the Tuesday night. It was also believed he may have been unaware that he was so badly injured because of the state of intoxication that he was in. It was unclear what he did between being stabbed and being found, which must have been a period of several hours.

A search was made of the area in which Mark was seen staggering in the hope of finding any clues to what was now a murder investigation. Several spots of blood were found at the bottom of Cock Inn yard and Lord Nelson yard. No weapon which could have been responsible for the injuries was found during the search.

News of the attack, and ultimately Mark's death, spread through the area quickly and it was during a conversation in a shopping arcade that a man who was to be regarded as a suspect was first considered to be suspicious. At around 6.45pm, a little over twelve hours after Mark was seen staggering through the streets, a man named George Sidney Hesketh, who was the caretaker of Guest's Arcade (also known as Barnsley Arcade), approached Herbert Heptinstall and asked him if he had heard that Mark had died. Heptinstall, a single 25-year-old billposter who lived at 31 Shambles Street, gave no response and walked away. Although

MINER FOUND FATALLY WOUNDED.

Barnsley Man Arrested in the Night.

CHARGE OF MURDER.

Period of Victim's Movements Unknown.

REMAND IN CUSTODY.

THERE was a swift sequel to the death in the Barnsley Beckett Hospital, last night, of Mark Scott, the man found wounded in a street at an early hour in the morning.

During the night the police arrested Herbert Heptinstall (25), single, a billposter, of 31, Shambles Street, Barnsley, and to-day he was brought before the borough magistrates charged with the wilful murder of Mark Scott (33), a miner, of 39, Albert Street.

The Court proceedings lasted only a few minutes, Heptinstall being remanded in custody after a brief statement by the Chief Constable (Mr. G. H. Butler).

The Chief Constable said the prisoner was charged with wilful murder and he had to ask for a remand for one week. He hoped then to be in a position to proceed with the charge.

"I may briefly relate the circumstances under which Scott was killed," he continued. "About quarter past six on Wednesday morning Police-constable Barraclough was on duty in Shambles Street when he was called by someone in the street and found Scott near the Windmill Yard. The man was in a state of collapse, and the officer found that he was wounded in the abdomen. He at once telephoned for the police ambulance and Scott was taken to the Beckett Hospital. During the day it was found necessary to perform an operation, but Scott died about 4.10 p.m."

MYSTERY OF NIGHT MOVEMENTS.

Mr. E. J. F. Rideal (one of the magistrates): The date in the charge is the 25th.

The Chief Constable: Yes, sir; it is supposed that the man's injuries were inflicted on Tuesday night.

Proceeding, the Chief Constable said. "Inquiries were made by the police, and prisoner is now charged with this offence. He was seen in Graham's Orchard on Tuesday night. We shall be able to produce evidence so far as violence is concerned inflicted by the prisoner. Scott was found near the place where he was assaulted. Where he had been during the night after this is alleged to have been done we do not know at present."

The Chairman (Mr. C. Plumpton): Prisoner will be remanded for one week.

An article from the Yorkshire Telegraph and Star *relating to the murder of Mark Scott.* (The author's collection)

this was unusual behaviour it did not come to the attention of the police until after Heptinstall was later arrested.

Heptinstall only became a suspect when he approached the police himself later that evening. Until this time there had been no reason for the police to consider the billposter in relation to the crime.

It was at around 9.40pm that Detective Inspector Hodgson and Inspector Herbert met Heptinstall, and they were soon to realise the potential significance of him when, after being asked a few questions, they were told: 'Between 10pm and 10.30pm on Tuesday August 25th I saw a man I know as Scott at the top of Graham's Orchard. He was drunk and shouting and using obscene language. I went past him and then turned round. He called me a ———, made to strike me and I struck him once in the stomach with my right hand, and tried to strike him on the face with my left, and then went away into Shambles Street. The last I saw of Scott was when he was standing there swearing.'

With such an admission made, despite his assertion that Mark Scott was still alive and with no mention made of a knife having been used during the fight, it was inevitable that Heptinstall would be regarded as a suspect and so he was duly arrested by Inspector Hodgson and charged with the murder. When charged the suspect replied, 'Wilful murder is ridiculous'.

Heptinstall was brought before the magistrates at Barnsley Borough Court the following day. The proceedings were very brief, lasting only a few minutes, and consisting simply of the cause of death and a general account of the circumstances of the discovery of the dying man, read by the Chief Constable G. H. Butler who argued there was sufficient evidence linking the accused to the crime because of the assault by Heptinstall which took place so close to where Mark was found wounded.

The Chief Constable made a request that the accused should be remanded in custody for a week, following which time he hoped to have the case at an adequate stage to progress it further towards the Assizes. The Chairman of the magistrates, Mr C. Plumpton allowed the request and Heptinstall was placed on remand.

The inquest into the death opened on 28 August and was presided over by the coroner, C. J. Howarth. The proceedings were again very brief and consisted of the basic facts of the case as they were understood at the time. Heptinstall, who was not present, had been charged with wilful murder, the coroner was told.

Adjourning the inquest to allow for legal proceedings to continue, Howarth told those present: 'I don't think it will be any good asking questions at the present time. An arrest has been made in connection with this man's death. Therefore I shall adjourn this inquiry until September 17th to see what transpires. Whether I shall require the services of the jury on that occasion I cannot tell.'

On 17 September the court reconvened but was again adjourned for another week. Major J. G. E. Rideal asked for another week on behalf of the Public Prosecutor and so the proceedings were adjourned until 2 October and took place before the Magistrates at Barnsley Borough Court, with the hearing lasting five-and-a-half hours. The hearing was to establish whether there was sufficient evidence in order to send Heptinstall to trial for Mark Scott's murder.

There was much interest in the hearing, with a queue of people wanting to observe proceedings extending more than a hundred yards. As a result, most of those wanting to gain admission to the court were unable to do so and instead formed a crowd which remained outside.

Major Rideal told the magistrates that on the night before Mark was found, there had been an altercation in Shambles Street between the accused and the victim as admitted by Heptinstall. This seemed to have begun when Mark shouted an obscene expression, directed at Heptinstall, who was heard to exclaim 'Oh!' Mark then attempted to kick Heptinstall but was unable to do so because he moved out of the way and kicked Mark twice with his right foot, causing him to fall to the ground. 'Go on! Give us a chance!' Mark shouted as Heptinstall was seen to walk away towards his home nearby.

The major argued that Heptinstall had access to a knife such as that which inflicted the wounds on the deceased, for he had been lodging at a fish shop in Shambles Street and had assisted the owners with preparing the fish and potatoes. But it was likely many other residents in the area either owned a knife or had access to one. The fact that Heptinsall had access to a sharp knife does not prove his involvement in a knife murder, especially given that the murder weapon was never found, and so its provenance could not be established. However, the knowledge that Heptinstall had been engaged in a violent altercation with Scott so soon before his death showed there was malice between the two men and therefore a motive for the billposter to kill him.

The owner of the fish shop, Francesco Carnevale, told the court that Heptinstall had been lodging there with him and his wife since Whitsuntide. Mark was in the shop on the Monday when Heptinstall entered. On seeing the billposter, Mark said to Carnevale: 'Frank, are you going to have this silly ——— as your son-in-law?' There was, however, no violence on this occasion and indeed, Heptinstall did not respond to the insult.

There were other individuals with a possible motive to commit murder, however. It was discovered that Mark Scott was a member of a gang known as the Cross School Gang. (Unfortunately information relating to this gang could not be obtained for this book, despite lengthy research. Perhaps the name of the gang relates to the former White Cross School in Barnsley.) It was unclear what Mark's position in the gang was, though his membership was not in dispute. Mary Smith confirmed he was in the gang but she did not know if he was leader.

Mary was also able to give some account of Mark's movements prior to the attack. He had arrived home at 5.30pm and was at that time heavily drunk. He ate tea and then left again, at around 7pm, with a man named Patrick Butler. Mary had waited up for him until 1am but had then gone to bed, believing Mark had stayed the night with friends. It was during the Barnsley Feast and so it was likely Mark would have been out drinking heavily. The feast was an annual event held during the last week of August and no doubt in 1931 it helped alleviate some of the worries and strains suffered during the onset of the worst recession in our country's history. The feast marked the annual temporary closure of the pits, allowing the workers to have a week off. The large outdoor market would be taken down and a large fairground was erected there. Other highlights included bringing the ponies out of the pits, with workers able to ride them to their resting field.

The fight between Mark and Heptinstall, outlined by the accused in his statement to the police, was witnessed by George Hesketh who told the court that neither man had a knife in his hand. 'They were not close enough to use one,' he said. This is not to say that Heptinstall did not return home, obtain a knife and hunt out Mark later in the night. The incident, Hesketh believed, had begun at around 9.40pm in Graham's Orchard, off Shambles Street, as Mark walked passed him. Mark was heard to make several obscene expressions and said, 'I will get the ——— yet.' Heptinstall was then spotted and Mark directed 'several filthy expressions' towards him. He then took a flying kick at Heptinstall, who managed to move out of the way in time. He then buttoned up his coat, said 'Oh' and retaliated.

The defence, led by Mr A. Smith, said that lamentably for the prosecution there was no actual evidence which linked the accused to the crime. Whilst Heptinstall had engaged in a brief violent scuffle with the deceased, there had been no knife involved and the fatal injuries were not inflicted during the scuffle. 'There has never been a case where the evidence for the prosecution was so conflicting and trifling,' he said.

Magistrate Herbert Smith considered the arguments and announced: 'After going carefully into the evidence I am satisfied within myself that no prima facie case has been made out and the prisoner will be discharged.'

The discharge of Heptinstall was greeted by wild cheering from many of those within the court. As he walked from the dock he was kissed by relatives and other well-wishers. Outside the court house the large crowd was cheering and Heptinstall's hand was shaken by large numbers of men. Women were seen to be crying hysterically.

Did Heptinstall hunt out Mark Scott later in the night, continuing the fight and was therefore wrongly acquitted? Or was Mark murdered because of his activities in the Cross School Gang? After Heptinstall left the dock to the delight of all those who had come to support him, the police in Barnsley got no closer to solving this murder mystery. At the eventual conclusion of the inquest the members of the jury, on the advice of the coroner, returned a verdict that Mark Scott was murdered by some person unknown.

CHAPTER 5

Murder of a Musician:
The Death of Lily Stephenson
(1962)

The trial of James Hanratty, the infamous 'M6 Murderer' fascinated people across Britain in the spring of 1962. It has proved to be controversial ever since, with many believing the wrong man was hanged for the murder of Michael Gregsten and attempted murder of Valerie Storey. But while Hanratty's trial was underway police in South Yorkshire were baffled by a violent killer in the mining town of Barnsley. Unlike the Hanratty case however, no man was ever to be captured, and the passage of five decades has not resolved the mystery of who killed Lily Stephenson whose body was found on Wednesday, 31 January 1962, at Springfield Place, a short distance outside the town centre of Barnsley.

Springfield Place, Barnsley where Lily Stephenson lived and was killed. (The author)

When she failed to return home after a shopping trip Lily's husband began to be concerned. His worries grew when he looked outside his home the following morning and saw his wife's shopping bag on the ground but could not see anything else. Daring not to investigate further on account of having a weak heart, he contacted the police. Detective Constable Clifford Chatterton and Detective Inspector Harold Riley were soon on the scene, and at around 11am that day they made a grim discovery. As they entered the small yard at Springfield Place, approximately a hundred yards from the Stephenson's home, Lily's body was clearly visible. She was in a crouched position but the full circumstances of her death were not revealed during the early weeks of the investigation. Years later the police stated that she had died as a result of blunt force trauma. In 1964 *The Star* printed an article about the murder of Anne Dunwell (discussed in the next chapter) which referred to Lily Stephenson's murder as a sex crime. My research has not confirmed whether this is true or merely mistaken journalism, but it is unusual that the police refused to discuss the cause of death in 1962.

The area had already featured in the annals of criminal history. In June 1953 a German woman named Charlotte Ball had been murdered in a house only 25 yards from where Lily's body was found. That murder had been committed by a Polish miner named Wilhelm Lubina who was a lodger at the Ball home, 15 Springfield Street. Lubina's guilt was never in question; he was caught in the act of murder by the victim's husband and he made a confession to the police. There was no connection, therefore, with Lubina having been convicted and executed eight years before Lily's death. It was also not a copycat murder because the two crimes were very different in how they were perpetrated.

With the police refusing to reveal the cause of death during the active period of the investigation, there was great speculation as to what had taken place. Lily's son-in-law, Lawrence Heywood, who identified the body, said she had generally been in good health. She did, however, suffer occasional attacks of pleurisy which was a particular problem during the winter months. She had been complaining about this health problem in recent weeks, Heywood said, but was too 'stubborn' to go and see a doctor. Any belief that death could have been from natural causes was far from the truth.

Following the discovery of Lily Stephenson's body, her 68-year-old husband, Albert, to whom she had been married since 1920, was taken to the police station. Detectives were anxious to make it known that he was 'certainly not under suspicion' for his wife's murder, but that he was merely there to assist them with their enquiries by helping to build up a complete picture of his wife. They also, no doubt, thought that Albert's staying so close to the crime scene would have added to the trauma he had already experienced.

Lily Stephenson was a 61-year-old club pianist. During the Second World War she had played for the Entertainments National Service Association (ENSA), providing entertainment for armed forces personnel. Lily had been well known on the stage since 1924 and was known as 'Lila' in professional circles. She was a regular pianist at weekends in working men's clubs and pubs, playing popular and classical music. Her last performance was at a club in Grimethorpe, near Barnsley, where a member recalled that she was 'a happy go lucky type of person who everybody liked'. Her daughter agreed, saying, 'She was a very placid person who wouldn't harm anybody and she was liked by everybody.' Lily lived with her husband in Springfield Street and was an avid reader of Western novels.

Scotland Yard was drafted into the investigation from the outset. This was common practice for many forces until very recent times, and occasionally continues today, particularly in large and complex cases because the Metropolitan Police Force has greater experience of murder investigations and greater resources at its disposal. The investigation was headed by Detective Superintendent John MacKay and Detective Sergeant Ashby of the Yard. All leave was cancelled for the dozens of officers working on the hunt for Lily's killer.

Although the cause of death could not be established at an early stage, according to the police there was no doubt from the outset that it was indeed a murder case with Detective Superintendent John Mackay stating: 'We are investigating the case on the assumption that it is murder.'

MacKay and Detective Sergeant Ashby held a conference with senior members of Barnsley CID to create an investigation strategy sharing knowledge and expertise. Such conferences are common in complex investigations.

Barnsley police station, where detectives worked from in their hunt for Lily Stephenson's killer. (The author)

During the post-mortem, carried out by Dr David Price, the time of death could not be established. But detectives quickly ascertained Lily's movements up until 5.35pm on the day before her body was found, and police appealed for anyone who might have seen her after 5.35pm to come forward and contact Chief Constable George Parfitt or any other police officer. 'We have many inquiries to make,' the Chief Constable told the press.

Lily had left her home at around 4.50pm on the Tuesday afternoon and was last seen in Springfield Street. She was wearing a navy-blue overcoat, black fur-lined boots and a blue scarf and was carrying two shopping bags. Lily was 5ft 3in tall, very slim with a fresh complexion and grey permanently waved hair. It would have been useful for a recent photograph to accompany the appeal but instead only a picture of Lily during her ENSA days was used.

I am always amazed at how some stories of no local interest are featured prominently in local newspapers. Although in the past many more households than present regularly read a newspaper (with newspapers being the main news source in the days when there were only two television channels in this country), generally local papers had to provide local news but also a round up of national and international news. Nonetheless, it was often the case that stories relating to incidents abroad would be printed on the front page whilst important local matters were squeezed into the other pages – if they were even featured at all. On 3 February an appeal for information from Lily's widower was printed in *The Star* but it may have gone unnoticed due to the main story in that day's paper about a prison riot in Paris. In the appeal Albert Stephenson said: 'If anyone can help find the person responsible for my wife's death I plead with them to help the police. I want the person, whoever it is, to be found.'

Plainclothes officers worked up to fifteen hours each day in the biggest murder investigation to take place in Barnsley at the time. Local houses and businesses were visited where people were asked if they had seen the dead woman at any time during those missing hours, or if they had seen anything which might have a bearing on the case. Local public houses, bars and working men's clubs were visited with an overt police presence every weekend to question regulars, but undercover police also visited in the hope of over-hearing rumours or suspicions. There was a frustratingly low level of information forthcoming, however, which led Superintendent MacKay to make a somewhat downcast statement to the press on 3 February: 'There is no development of any sort at all. Routine inquiries are proceeding and it is just a process of elimination.'

Soon into the investigation one piece of interesting information was given to the police, though it may have had no relevance. It emerged that the enclosed yard in which Lily's body was found opened on to a narrow alleyway which attracted courting couples, many of whom were engaging in undesirable behaviour. The residents claimed they often had to ask the couples to go away.

Another, curious, piece of information was derived from two children, aged four and five years old, who had been playing in the yard hours before Lily's body was found there. They had not noticed the body or anything amiss in the yard despite having played in it for some time. This begs the question of where Lily was at this time. If alive why did she not return home the previous evening? If she was dead then where was her body?

When the inquest opened on 2 February the cause of death had still not been fully established according to Detective Constable

Clifford Chatterton. The inquest was adjourned by the coroner, S. H. B. Gill, pending further investigation.

With no breakthrough a week into the investigation, 12 detectives from West Ridings CID were brought in to assist by bolstering the number of police involved. With the additional manpower the scale of the house-to-house enquiries was increased. Originally, only houses within half a mile of the crime scene were visited but this area was increased. Plain clothes detectives and officers attended Lily's funeral to observe the behaviour of any suspects who might attend, to observe any other behaviour and to overhear any conversations which might have a bearing on the case.

On 9 February the Chairman of Barnsley Football Club, Joe Richards, who was also a Justice of the Peace, made an appeal over the loudspeaker before a match began at the Barnsley stadium. That same day an announcement was made at the Dillington Park greyhound track. That weekend the clergy of the local churches made appeals during their sermons and the police continued their visits of the local drinking establishments, making appeals at clubs and also the local cinemas.

The police were particularly keen to trace two men seen eating out of paper bags, who were seen walking along Dodsworth Road between Town End and Springfield Street between 5.30pm and

Dodsworth Road in Barnsley where two men were seen walking shortly after it was believed Lily Stephenson was killed. (The author)

5.40pm on the Tuesday that Lily was last seen alive. The police had eliminated a motorcyclist, seen riding at great speed in the vicinity of the crime scene at around the same time, from their inquiries.

The manager of the Ritz cinema in Barnsley, Arthur Seddon, tried to campaign for businesses, organisations or individuals to offer a substantial reward for information. He was frustrated that no reward was offered.

The murder squad was also frustrated that its investigation was hampered by sizeable gaps in its knowledge of the victim. Friends and neighbours described Lily as a 'woman of mystery' and the detectives were surprised that many of her friends knew very little about her. 'She was always polite and sociable but she said very little,' one neighbour remarked.

On the night of 11 February tragedy was to hit Barnsley once again when a man was fatally wounded in the yard of a pub in the town. Roy Blakey, who was 18 years old and known locally as 'Dusty', died as a result of injuries sustained in a fight. Although the police expected to make an early arrest, the second murder in less than two weeks added extra pressure as some resources had to be diverted from the Lily Stephenson case. It was quickly announced that there was no connection to the two murders. The police were correct in their assertion of a quick arrest and on 14 February a local man, named Charles Anthony Dunn, appeared in court charged with Blakey's murder.

At around the same time, a third murder took place in Barnsley; the result of a domestic incident. In a period of only three weeks there had been three murders in the small town, along with murders in Sheffield, further showing that life in the 1960s was not as safe and crime free as many people like to recollect.

Meanwhile, the police were still having no luck finding the person who killed Lily and continued to inform the press that there were no new developments, which must have put Lily's killer at greater ease. Dissatisfied with the police, and fearing that the killer could strike again, Tom Walton, a 70-year-old former miner, tried to set up civilian patrols of the area. He told the press that the local population was in fear with a feeling of 'terror' and that patrols would enable people to leave their homes once again.

MacKay believed that the killer had managed to evade capture and suspicion because he was being shielded by someone. He announced on 17 February that he did not expect to make any arrests in the near future. The determination to capture the killer had not dissipated, he was anxious to say, and the police would continue visiting pubs and clubs at weekends in the hope of over-hearing 'bar gossip'. He also told the press that the cause of death was known but he would still not reveal it.

Two days later, however, the description of a new suspect was revealed. It was announced that the police wished to speak to a man aged around 30 years old, who was 5ft 4in to 5ft 5in tall, of slim build and with well-greased brown hair which was brushed back and slightly bushy. The man might have been wearing a dark suit with a white open neck shirt, blue pullover, a fawn 'shorty' overcoat and black shoes. Anyone who saw this man between 5.30pm and 7.30pm was encouraged to contact the police.

Despite this lead, the investigation began to be scaled down only three weeks after Lily's body was found. On 21 February it was announced that the detectives from the West Ridings force were returning to work in their own force area. Barnsley police claimed this reduction in manpower was 'not significant', but it would have eased the concerns of the killer even further as would the news, two days later, that MacKay and Ashby were returning to London for their first period of leave since the investigation began. Whilst there, they gave a report to their superiors and promised that they would return to Barnsley in order to continue the hunt for the killer.

As the detectives left Barnsley they hoped that one or two more witnesses would come forward, believing their evidence could potentially be sufficient to bring the murderer to justice. They again appealed for any information relevant to the investigation.

Sadly, these one or two witnesses never did come forward and so the man who murdered Lily Stephenson got away with his wicked crime.

And so, more than half a century after her death, the murder of Lily Stephenson remains the oldest of South Yorkshire's cold cases which it has listed as still worthy of reviewing. How long it will remain on that list is uncertain. There is still some hope, however, because despite so many years having passed it is still possible that the killer is still alive and that someone knows their identity. If the man described above was the killer, and the description of him being aged around 30 years old was accurate, then it is conceivable he could still be alive at the time of writing.

However, there is a problem in that the Metropolitan Police files, consisting of thousands of pages of witness statements and police reports, are open to public view at the National Archives. With so much information about Lily's murder now in the public domain there seems little prospect that the police will ever catch her killer. The police like to keep secrets about the murderer in order to trap a suspect into revealing something which is not in the public domain. With all the papers on public view there are no longer any secrets other than those held by the person who ended Lily's life all those years ago.

CHAPTER 6

A Beast at Large:
The Murder of Anne Dunwell
(1964)

nne Elizabeth Dunwell was just 13 years old when her life was tragically taken on Wednesday, 6 May 1964. She had visited her aunt, Irene Varah, in Bramley a few miles outside of Rotherham, where she had originally planned to spend the night because there was no school the following day as local elections meant her school was used as a polling station. But instead, Anne decided to catch the bus back to Whiston where she lived with her grandparents, at Sandringham Avenue. Her mother had died and her father lived in Attercliffe in Sheffield, seeing his daughter at weekends when she visited and collected her ten shilling pocket money. Her grandfather worked nights as a gate-keeper at Hadfield's steel manufacturers, but Anne was looking forward to seeing her grandmother, who she knew would be at home. That evening Anne had played with friends in the Howard Road area and went to a fish and chip shop, but by 9.15pm she was ready to return home. She headed to the bus stop near the Ball Inn, intending to catch the 9.29pm bus. Anne should have arrived home at 9.40pm but she never made it. She was seen waiting for the bus by several passers-by, but when asked at a later date, the driver and none of the bus passengers, including a group of bingo players, could recall the teenage girl who looked much younger than her years and was wearing a light-blue coat. It was later established that Anne never boarded the bus and she certainly never made it back to Whiston.

It was on the Thursday morning of Election Day that a man driving to work brought the awful crime to light. What initially appeared to lorry driver Tommy Williams to be a tailor's dummy was actually the partially-clothed body of a teenage girl dumped in one of the most undignified ways possible. It was at the bottom of a dung heap on farmland in Slade Hooton Lane, a winding country lane between Carr and Slade Hooton, three miles from Maltby. The shocking truth was realised when Williams returned half an hour later with his brother-in-law, Bill Poulter.

Williams described the discovery to reporters: 'I was driving down the lane when I saw what I thought was a tailor's dummy with its feet in the hedge and back on the manure heap. I thought it was a practical joke and I drove on. When I got to work I told my brother-in-law about what I had seen and to make sure we drove back. We went within two yards of the body which had a stocking round its neck, and noticed that the legs were badly bruised. There were also bruises on the face. The arms seemed as if they had been placed behind the back.' Williams added that there was no clothing visible and that there were no footprints or tyre tracks at the scene as far as he could tell.

It would take fifteen hours to establish the girl's identity. A distinctive silver medallion with religious engravings on it was found attached to the dead girl's wristwatch. Originally believing that the medallion had been deliberately left by the killer, the police asked local clergymen if they could identify it. But it transpired the medallion was not as significant as first thought. It had been found by Anne in a carpet returned from the cleaners and she had decided to keep it. A member of the public, however, heard about the medallion and approached the police to inform them that he knew its latest owner. This led detectives to the family of Anne Elizabeth Dunwell who were able to confirm that the dead girl was indeed the missing 13 year old. Anne's identity was confirmed 15 hours after the grim discovery.

A post-mortem later established that she had been sexually assaulted and then strangled with her own stockings, which were tied around her neck. Other items of clothing were missing.

The discovery sparked one of the largest murder investigations ever for the former West Ridings Constabulary who warned: 'We have a beast at large who has killed once and will possibly try to kill again.' But almost half a century later, the identity of the killer of Anne Dunwell, the teenage girl who had ambitions of becoming a hairdresser, was excited she would soon own her very own tape recorder, and who was described by her headmaster as being 'just an ordinary schoolgirl' remains a mystery.

The investigation back in 1964 was led by Detective Chief Superintendent Clifford Lodge, who wasted no time in gathering evidence and tracing potential witnesses. He set up a mobile police station close to where Anne should have caught the bus on that tragic night. The police activity led to large amounts of information being gathered quickly, and by 11 May, 3,000 statements had been taken. Detectives assumed that as Anne had not stepped foot on the bus she had been intending to catch, she had either been picked up at the bus stop or she had begun to walk home and had been picked up by her killer en route.

Lodge appealed for anyone who had seen Anne or anything suspicious, to come forward. He told a packed press conference on the Thursday night: 'Anyone who saw the girl at 9.15pm or between Howard Road, Bramley, and the bus stop opposite the Ball Inn, or anywhere in the Bramley, Maltby or Whiston areas should contact the police immediately.'

Several witnesses were able to provide information of vehicles seen in the area. Sadly, the significance of some of this information would not be recognised until 40 years later. At the time there was no evidence to strongly suggest any of the drivers of those vehicles were involved in Anne's murder, but detectives were keen to speak to them in order to establish whether they may have been responsible or may have seen something of relevance.

Parents were warned to be extra vigilant to protect their children who were, they claimed, very much in danger of a repeat of what was described by detectives as a 'dastardly, perverted criminal assault'. As the school holidays began towards the end of May, parents were asked to watch their children closely. 'If you see anything at all suspicious don't delay in informing us,' Detective Chief Superintendent Lodge told parents through the media. The Brownies and Girl Guides postponed their collection plans deciding that it was unwise for the girls to be visiting homes without adults accompanying them.

Two days after Anne was last seen alive, a 15-year-old girl waiting at a bus stop in Brinsworth, was accosted by a man in a white van who was acting strangely. He asked her for directions to Worksop but did not try to offer her a lift. Nonetheless, the girl felt concerned and her family reported the incident to the police. Was this the killer trying to approach another teenage girl or was this merely evidence of the fact that in 1964 young girls were offered lifts by men on an all-too-frequent basis?

Unfortunately, the incidence of strangers approaching children was all too common in an age of innocence which resulted in violent crimes across the country. Indeed, between 1963 and 1965 the Moors Murderers approached, abducted and killed five children, sexually assaulting at least four of them. Several other child attackers were active at the time and were responsible for abducting and killing their victims. The same year that Anne was murdered, for example, a 14-year-old girl named Jenny Tighe was abducted whilst waiting for a bus in Oldham. Unlike Anne, however, her body was never found. I am not suggesting the two cases are in any way connected – though they could be – but am simply saying that the 1960s were not as safe for teenage girls as nostalgia would have us believe.

Five days before Anne's murder a 14-year-old girl from nearby Canklow was offered ten shillings by a middle-aged male motorist if she would get in his car. The girl refused and told the man, who had grey hair, blue eyes and was wearing a brown suit, that she would call the police. He drove off quickly and was never caught, but not before he asked for directions to Maltby. One has to wonder if this man was responsible for Anne Dunwell's murder. It seems too much of a coincidence for there to be no connection. We can only speculate what could have happened to this teenage girl had she got inside the car. It is unfortunate that this story was not commonly known in the small South Yorkshire town. Had Anne known of what had happened to the 14 year old perhaps she would not have ventured away from her aunt's home that night.

A woman has recently spoken out about her belief she was accosted by Anne's killer. 'When I was 11, a bloke tried to get me to go with him and I ran away from him. A few months later Anne Dunwell was murdered about four miles away. She was a bit older than me. When the photofit and description of the man wanted for questioning were in the papers I realised it was the same man. The police know about it and I was given a name for the man about a year ago by someone I know so I e-mailed *Crimewatch*', she said.

Anne's father, Sam Dunwell, told the police and journalists that his daughter was unlikely to get into a stranger's car. 'I cannot believe that Anne would accept a lift in a car from a stranger,' he told David Sharpe, a journalist working for *The Star*. 'She travelled all over on her own. She was very independent like that. She would only go with someone she knew, never with a stranger. The person who did this terrible thing must be someone she knew and well, whoever it is, I appeal for him to come forward before he has the urge to strike again.'

A 13-year-old school friend of Anne's told a curious story to the police and media which suggested the possibility that Anne had actually been targeted and perhaps stalked by her killer. She was reported as telling a journalist that Anne was terrified of footsteps in the night. 'Anne was worried by footsteps and she thought she was being followed', the girl claimed. Anne had first told her friend about the night-time occurrences just after the Christmas of 1963; only months before she was murdered. On one occasion the girl was with Anne when they both heard footsteps outside her grandparents' home. On another occasion, Anne's grandfather also heard footsteps but did not see anyone. Anne told her friend that she had heard the footsteps on several nights. Was this a sign of the over-active imaginations of two teenage girls or was there someone hiding in the darkness around Anne's home?

A few people also came forward to tell detectives that they had occasionally seen men following women and indecently exposing themselves.

An appeal was made for courting couples to come forward if they were in the area and saw something of potential relevance. Anonymity was offered to encourage people to provide information. One such couple with possible relevant information did approach detectives. They said they had seen a man and a girl 'struggling' in a blue saloon car parked in a cul-de-sac at Slacks Lane, close to the Ball Inn, at 11pm on the night of Anne's death. The couple caught a fleeting glimpse in their car headlights as they drove by. The man was described as being aged around 19 years old with dark hair and sharp features. Although the lane was frequented by courting couples, these witnesses claimed this was 'certainly' a struggle and not some passionate behaviour. Was this a sighting of Anne and her killer or could it have been totally unconnected? If it was unconnected the 'struggling' couple certainly never came forward.

The police searched fields and country lanes in the area where Anne's body was found and used tracker dogs in a bid to locate Anne's missing clothing and a wicker basket with cane handle that she had been seen carrying on the night she died. After days of searching the police had no luck, but five days into the investigation their attention turned to Ulley Reservoir, just north of Swallownest and approximately six miles from where Anne's body was found. Two men walking around the reservoir had found some items of clothing at the edge of the water. This clothing was soon identified as being part of that worn by the teenager.

A specialist team of police divers from Nottingham searched the 50ft deep reservoir looking for other items and any other clues which could help the murder squad. After half an hour they began to have some success and found an item of underwear thought to have belonged to Anne, a bacon rasher and a milk bottle. A wicker basket, a crayon case and handkerchief which belonged to the dead girl were amongst other items retrieved.

It was only more than forty years after the murder that police revealed that the clothing found in the reservoir had been very dirty. Whilst the police have to keep some secrets in the hope that a suspect may incriminate themselves by revealing details not in the public domain, sometimes holding back information means family, friends, colleagues or acquaintances of a killer may fail to see what

Some of Anne's clothing and belongings were found by walkers and police divers at Ulley Reservoir. (The author)

could be a vital clue. Some of the dirt, such as silt, came from the reservoir. However, other dirt on the clothing suggested Anne might have been in an area where there was foundry slag and/or coal dust at around the time of her death. It is quite possible she was killed in the back of a vehicle or building which contained such materials before her killer disposed of her body and clothing.

'The overall indication suggests that this was probably in the back of a van used to carry coal or slag, or in an out-building such as a coal house or garage. Having said that I don't rule anything out,' the press were told. If this information had been revealed in 1964 who knows what impact it may have had? Perhaps suspicions may have been cast upon a person with access to a vehicle or garage containing coal or slag, and any such individual acting out of character following the murder may have caused suspicion in the minds of those who knew them, resulting in information coming to the attention of the murder detectives. Revealing this detail after so many decades may have been a mistake. However, it should be remembered that South Yorkshire was a highly industrial part of the country in 1964.

Despite a thorough search of the reservoir and surrounding areas, some items of Anne's clothing were not recovered, but this was not revealed until 2002. A half-inch button from her cardigan and a gold sleeper earring were not found. It seems likely they were lost during a struggle and went missing at the location where the terrible crime was committed. Indeed, Detective Superintendent Ernie Roper, who led the re-opened investigation, expressed his belief that they were lost at the crime scene. It was hoped they may have been found by someone who knew the killer and this is very possibly the case, but the chances of someone remembering after 38 years was unlikely.

As the investigation continued, Anne's funeral took place on 13 May with her being buried in the same grave as her mother at a Sheffield cemetery. Anne's sister, Irene, who was 18 at the time, had to be carried away from the grave after she collapsed through the emotional turmoil her family were experiencing. Anne's grandmother had suffered a nervous breakdown and over the years to come her father would suffer tremendously. The route which the funeral entourage followed was lined by members of the public horrified by the wicked crime. Detectives mingled with the crowds in the hope and belief that the killer was present, or that some clue might have been forthcoming from unusual behaviour or comments made in conversation. If the killer *was* present out of an act of remorse or to heighten his experience of his crime, the detectives were unaware.

On the day of the funeral police officers also watched the route between where Anne was last seen and where her body was found. They spoke to all motorists they encountered and took statements where appropriate. It was their hope that people who regularly travelled in the area may have been driving those same lanes on the night of Anne's death. Detective Chief Superintendent Lodge told the press of his hopes that these activities would generate important information: 'Although we have taken several thousand statements from people in the Bramley area we are hoping that these inquiries will give us a definite lead,' he said.

On 18 May Detectives mingled with visitors to Wickersley Show, an annual agricultural show. By this time they announced they had spoken to approximately 10,000 members of the public, but were still seeking the evidence to nail the killer. Chief Superintendent Charles Woodham, Head of Rotherham Division, told the press: 'Our inquiries are being pushed steadily ahead, coldly and clinically, with checking and cross checking. And all the time the prospects of getting the man we want strengthens.'

Nineteen days after the murder an identikit picture was printed in the local press. It was of a man who called himself Pete, who drove a dark grey Mini van and who offered lifts to young girls, some of whom were known to Anne Dunwell. The man was described as being aged between 21 and 27, approximately 5ft 5in to 5ft 6in tall, of medium build and with a long thin face and nose. He had pock marks on his

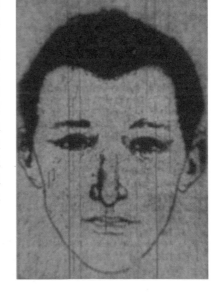

Detectives in 1964 were keen to speak to a man calling himself 'Pete' in relation to Anne's murder. They issued this photofit image of him. (The author's collection)

cheeks, was clean-shaven and had mousy, dark-brown hair with a 'widow's peak', which was wavy, short, and brushed back.

Within hours of the picture's release an anonymous caller phoned the police incident room. The caller named one of his neighbours as being the person shown in the image and the police confirmed they were making 'detailed inquiries' as a result of the call. Identikit pictures, much like the modern day e-fits, are often based on rather vague descriptions and often resembled the appearance of many individuals. Consequently, several names were given to the police but none of them resulted in any arrests. Pete's identity remains uncertain.

When undertaking any major investigation the police have to consider other crimes which may be linked to their own case. Detective Chief Inspector Lodge confirmed to the press that they were not linking the murder of Anne Dunwell to any other sex crimes perpetrated in the region, including the murder of Lily Stephenson and the infamous Bubble Car Murders of Chesterfield (often referred to as the Carbon Copy murders).

Unfortunately, despite the best efforts of the police, with more than 30,000 people being spoken to in what was the largest investigation of the West Ridings region for the time, detectives drew a blank and active work of the hunt for Anne's killer slowly ground to a halt. The murderer must have become more relaxed and eventually aware that he had probably managed to get away with murder.

In June 2002 South Yorkshire Police announced they had re-opened the investigation, and in doing so, they acknowledged the probability Anne's killer was now dead. But they expressed their desire to solve the case for the sake of her family, in particular her elderly father, whose lives had inevitably been traumatised 'We are determined now as our colleagues were, to identify the killer,' Detective Superintendent Ernie Roper told the press when revealing details of the new investigation he was leading. The work to be undertaken, he said, would be a forensic and documentary review from the 1964 investigation. This work had actually begun the previous year but the police did not want to raise any hopes for Anne's family without good reason. 'I am very positive about the work that we're doing and we still have true potential to identify Anne's killer,' Roper said when making the announcement. He added: 'I have been working with a small team of officers and the

Forensic Science Service over the past year to re-examine case papers and material relating to the murder of Anne Dunwell. I am now awaiting the results of scientific work being carried out by forensics on exhibits recovered in 1964. I will announce these results as soon as information is available.'

Using modern police techniques and technology to re-investigate old crimes can, and often does, bring dividends, but with the knowledge that new information can still be obtained, even decades after a crime, an appeal was made for anyone who had failed to come forward back in 1964.

Roper continued: 'I would appeal for anyone with any information in relation to Anne's murder to come forward. It is possible even 38 years on that someone has withheld vital information for good reasons but perhaps feel safe and confident passing that on today. I am sure someone will know something and we have even had three of four calls relating to the matter over the past few months. A trained family liaison officer is in regular contact with Anne's sister and her husband who are aware of the current situation.'

Anne's sister, Irene, also made an appeal to a packed press conference at the South Yorkshire Police Headquarters:

'I promise Anne every time I visit her grave that one day her killer will be found and brought to justice. I know it will never bring her back but it will let her be at peace after all these years. We have had this pain and this hurt for 38 years; it is never going to go away, just like our memories of Anne will never go away. We have been robbed of seeing Anne grow up, get married and have children. She was only a child. She did not deserve to die like this.'

Amazingly, new witnesses began to come forward. A woman who was 15 in 1964, and who knew Anne from school, informed detectives that she had seen Anne at 9.45pm. At that time Anne was in Wickersley walking along Bawtry Road near Marcliffe Crescent heading towards Whiston. This proved that Anne had not boarded the bus and had probably been abducted as she walked towards her grandparents' home. This had long been suspected, but there was never the evidence to say for certain that this was what happened. 'Based on this sighting it is quite clear to me that Anne may well have been abducted somewhere on the main road between Wickersley and her home in Whiston,' Detective Superintendent

Roper told the media. This was important information and goes to show that even after decades, appeals for information can still reap rewards.

Anne's murderer may have taken care to escape justice for decades but there was something he could not have anticipated back in the 1960s because it had not existed at that time. Using the latest DNA technology it was hoped that Anne's killer may have left a forensic trace that could be used to link him, without doubt, to his crime. A series of rapes unconnected to Anne's murder, which took place between 1983 and 1986, had been solved due to advances in DNA technology and it was believed that similar results could be obtained in sex murders such as the murder of Anne Dunwell. Detectives were justified in their optimism.

By examining the knots in the stockings used to strangle Anne, fibres from her clothing and some bacteria on her underwear, forensic scientists were able to find some staggering information about the man detectives had long been hunting. In addition to finding a trace of DNA which could be compared to the DNA of suspects, a trace of bacteria was found within the semen. The bacterium was Neisseria gonorrhoea which showed Anne's killer suffered from the sexually transmitted disease gonorrhoea. When run through the database of offenders the DNA did not match any convicted criminal on the database.

Subsequent advances in DNA technology further increased the hopes of the murder squad. Detective Sergeant Sue Hickman expressed her optimism about the DNA evidence potentially solving the murder by saying, 'This is a very exciting development and I hope that it will finally give Anne's family the closure they deserve. Innocent people have nothing to fear from this enquiry as we can conclusively eliminate anyone who is not the offender. The only person with anything to fear is the individual who sexually abused and murdered Anne Elizabeth Dunwell.'

Anyone with suspicions about a friend, relative, acquaintance or neighbour could contact the police and the individual would easily be eliminated by DNA if they were not involved.

Police officers took mouth swabs to test suspects from the original investigation and close relatives of suspects who had since died, to find close family matches. ('The real killer of Lynette White, a Cardiff prostitute for whose murder three men were wrongly convicted, was identified when DNA from the crime scene was found to match that of a close relative of the murderer.)

By using the DNA to eliminate innocent people, detectives were able to reduce the number of suspects. Detectives announced that all original suspects still alive, whose identities were known, had been traced and been fully cooperative in giving a sample of their DNA. Many original suspects were therefore quickly eliminated, and eventually detectives felt confident the murderer was one of only 12 men on their list of suspects. No doubt those eliminated felt a tremendous amount of relief because although they would of course have known their innocence, the finger of suspicion can often linger while a murder remains unsolved.

Detective Sergeant Hickman added: 'We're working very closely on this investigation with the Forensic Science Service and the Home Office Police Standards Unit, which are supporting cold cases around the country as part of a national operation. Cases like this one will never be closed until the culprit is known.'

Roper told the conference that in addition to suffering from gonorrhoea, Anne's killer was likely to have local connections, was possibly an acquaintance of Anne's, probably had a criminal record and used a grey or green van. 'By linking all these aspects together we're hoping the public will give us a name,' Roper said, but he added, 'We are not going to trawl through records, but if someone fits this profile we'll conduct some thorough research.' It seemed very possible that someone would know the murderer's identity given his medical condition.

In their determination to solve the case detectives turned to something which had not existed in 1964 when there were only two television channels. They decided to make a national appeal through the BBC's *Crimewatch UK* in the firm belief that fresh information could still be uncovered even after so many years had passed. Appeals through the local and regional media had resulted in some new information being revealed to detectives but it was felt there would be even more information forthcoming if they could carry out a major nationwide television appeal.

'All the previous press appeals have resulted in fresh information being provided by the public. Most of this information has never been passed to the police before. I am confident that the *Crimewatch* appeal will result in more new information to help us solve this case,' Roper said. He was also quoted as saying: 'The investigation into the murder of Anne Dunwell is still very much an active investigation and the team of detectives involved are pursuing hundreds of actions linked to several lines of enquiry.'

On 26 March 2003 Detective Superintendent Roper made such an appeal on the *Crimewatch* programme and a reconstruction of Anne's last known movements was broadcast. Amazingly, it generated more than 170 calls, naming 65 new possible suspects, some of whom were considered to be of interest to the murder squad. The police confirmed the information was relevant to the investigation and that the 65 men, if still alive, would be visited by officers and that DNA swabs would be requested from each of them. 'I remain absolutely convinced that at least one member of the public knows the identity of Anne Dunwell's killer. If you are that person and you have not already contacted us, we urge you to do so now. We will relentlessly pursue those lines of inquiry to identify the person responsible for killing Anne,' Roper said after the programme.

Thirty-five names were of particular interest to detectives and the police announced they would all be asked to give a DNA sample. Following the programme a police spokesperson said: 'We are very grateful to the public. The response has been fantastic. We have 35 names and we'll be knocking on doors soon.'

Momentum was not lost as Detective Superintendent Roper and his team worked their way through the new information, comparing it with information from the original investigation where appropriate, and a little over a year after the *Crimewatch* appeal detectives were able to build up a good picture of the man they believed committed the crime more than forty years earlier.

Given that the killer was believed to have suffered from gonorrhoea it was felt that hospital records could assist with the murder hunt because if the killer knew of his condition he may well have been seeking treatment for it at Rotherham District General Hospital. The killer would have required treatment because symptoms begin to manifest themselves between four and six days of infection. The symptoms for men include a burning sensation during urination and discharge. If left untreated the infection can cause epididymitis (which causes testicular pain and pain and swelling of the scrotum), pelvic inflammatory disease, or affect valves and joints throughout the body. Therefore, Anne's killer would have required treatment in the Rotherham area if indeed he lived in the area. Detectives, however, met with a hurdle due to patient confidentiality. Historic medical records were sought for all of those who were being treated for the disease but hospital bosses refused to cooperate claiming that to do so would be a breach of human rights and would breach legislation. Irene Hall, Anne's sister, was furious at what she called 'political correctness gone mad' where the interests of a killer's privacy outweighed the interests of justice. 'The police are closer to solving Anne's murder than ever before, and yet all the hospital can do is talk about patient confidentiality. It's as though the killer has got rights, and Anne hasn't got any at all,' Mrs Hall said. 'We don't seem to have the law on our side; the offender seems to have the law on his side.'

Rotherham NHS Trust said they had considered the request at length and had sought legal advice about how the law stands regarding releasing confidential information. 'While the trust would wish to see the perpetrator of the crime apprehended and convicted, the professional advice is that the patient information should not be released in this instance,' an official told the police.

A detective described this decision as 'frustrating' stating that the number of suspects had been reduced to such a small number that if the hospital cooperated there was a high possibility that the killer's identity could be established beyond reasonable doubt.

Talks were had between the police and the NHS and questions were asked in the House of Commons in order to overcome the legal issues in the interests of justice.

Despite the difficulties in obtaining information from medical records, the police had been able to progress the investigation. Frustratingly, most of the information pointing to Anne's killer was in the possession of the police from an early stage in the investigation and was even reported about in the newspapers of the time. However, in the days before computer systems it was a matter of linking information written on police record cards and many pieces of information would never be connected to each other so their full significance was never appreciated. It was this old system of police work which enabled Peter Sutcliffe, the Yorkshire Ripper, to remain at large despite the police having questioned him on several occasions and despite several pieces of information pointing towards his guilt. Individually, these were explained away by the serial killer but if they had been grouped together then an arrest would have been highly likely. It was only when all of the information in the Anne Dunwell murder was put into a modern computer system known as HOLMES (Home Office Large Major Enquiry System) that the connections began to be seen. And of course, the DNA evidence was able to eliminate suspects, enabling police to concentrate their resources on the most important leads and locating and investigating individuals who had never been traced.

Amongst the new information which the police obtained through their modern day appeals were details of vehicles seen in the area on the night of the murder. Some of this new information complimented that obtained in 1964 and elevated its significance.

A man driving from Brookhouse to his home in Carr on the night of the murder saw a small grey or light green van with rear windows as he reached the junction with Carr Lane. The van was parked on a small track called Green Lane near a disused mill, at around 10pm or 10.15pm. It was only approximately two hundred yards away from where Anne's body was later found. Thus, this sighting was highly significant, being made in close proximity to where the killer left Anne's body and so soon after she was last seen alive.

Roper appealed for further information about this vehicle and its driver who had never come forward. 'Dozens of grey vans were checked in 1964 but I would appeal to anyone with any information as to who may have been in such a van near the disused windmill at Carr on that Wednesday night in 1964 to come forward,' he said.

Who was the driver of this vehicle and why has that individual not come forward? Could Anne have been inside the vehicle at this time? It is unfortunate that this information was not known about in 1964.

The description of the vehicle seen on Green Lane was similar to a vehicle described by other witnesses who saw a Mini van in the Whiston and Bramley areas.

Roper said: 'Following fresh information received only last week, I would like to make an appeal in relation to three sightings of a Mini-type van. We believe that the sightings relate to the same vehicle and that the van was in the possession of Anne's killer.' He added, 'I make an appeal to anyone able to associate this type of vehicle with a male who regularly wore shiny cufflinks and who came from the Bramley area of Rotherham to contact the incident room.' The significance of the cufflinks will soon be discussed.

Roper said it was likely the killer would have had a criminal record, that Anne probably knew her killer, and that he had strong local connections.

Detective Sergeant Hickman said: 'Any relevant information received is valued by the team as it helps us create a picture of life in the area in 1964,' and she appealed for information about other cars not traced during the original investigation, which were seen on the night of the murder.

A grey/blue Morris Minor-type van was seen by a group of girl guides. It was parked outside the Welfare Hall, Cross Street, at about 9.30pm.

A white man was sat in the driver's seat. He was leaning on the steering wheel whilst looking out of the front window towards the Ball Inn pub area at the crossroads where Anne was seen waiting for her bus.

Two women saw a black car, believed to have been a Humber Hawk or Super Snipe with a distinctive large patch of green paint on the front or rear offside wing at about 9.20pm. Three young men were in this car, which was parked at Cross Street. The men were all sitting in the front. The driver of the vehicle was white, had long blond hair and was wearing a white shirt.

Importantly, the two women outside Jackson's shop on Cross Street also saw a girl who may have been Anne Dunwell walking along Cross Street towards the Ball Inn at the same time. They also saw her standing at the bus stop where Anne should have got on the bus. As the women boarded their bus they noticed that the vehicle had moved from Cross Street and was now on Bawtry Road, parked very close to where Anne was stood at the stop from where she hoped to get on the bus home. Did the girl get into the car? If the girl was Anne and she did get into the car, does this explain why she never got on her bus? If the girl was Anne, and it seems likely that it was, then even if the three men were not involved in the murder they may have been important witnesses who saw Anne very shortly before she met her killer, but were too afraid to come forward at the time. It was certainly an important sighting and the three men involved have still not come forward.

This same vehicle, or one very similar, was seen by another witness. It was parked near Hall School in Maltby on the night Anne was killed.

Despite the other vehicles in the area, police concentrated on the sightings of the green or grey Mini van during the re-investigation for they believed it was driven by Anne's killer – a man who wore shiny cufflinks – and was used to transport her body to Slade Hooton Lane.

Forty years after the murder a witness who had been spoken to in 1964 was questioned again about their statement and, despite the passage of time, was able to provide additional information which pointed strongly towards a man who would become the prime suspect in the murder.

In addition to repeating the story of a girl approaching a van close to the Ball Inn pub, the witness told the detectives that the driver of the vehicle was wearing shiny cufflinks. She remembered that the cufflinks had shone when catching the light. This tiny detail was probably not considered significant back in 1964 but its importance could not be underestimated. Detectives were now convinced that the girl was indeed Anne and that the man with the shiny cufflinks was her killer. Remarking upon this new revelation, Detective Sergeant Sue Hickman said: 'This new piece of information is extremely significant for us. It matches previous information we had about the vehicle on Cross Street and where Anne's body was found. There were not too many people in those days who wore cufflinks so it's very good information for us.'

The cufflinks may not have been mentioned in 1964 by this particular witness, but other witnesses did remark upon a man who aroused suspicions and who wore cufflinks.

The cufflinks were described as simply being 'shiny' in articles relating to the renewed murder hunt in the twenty-first century, but detectives knew the cufflinks in far greater detail. Back in 1964 they were described as having a gold surround with a red design of a woman carrying an open umbrella. Thus, they were highly distinctive – more so than the vast number of 'shiny cufflinks' around today and all of those in existence over the past five decades. The cufflinks might still exist and be in someone's possession. If so, their provenance could be established. Perhaps then, the police made a mistake by referring to them simply as being 'shiny' in appeals made in the media. It is unfortunate they have neglected to provide the full details of this case, merely giving the public a watered down version and hoping that this is sufficient to jog memories. The cufflinks were of relevance because they drew the attention of the police back to a man who was to become their prime suspect.

The man was also described back in 1964 as wearing a gold wristwatch with a round black face, gold numerals and hands, and a gold expanding bracelet. Again, the information relating to the watch and bracelet was omitted from information later released by the police.

There was also a Scottish man seen in the area – at the Ball Inn, Bramley – a week before Anne's murder who aroused suspicion and generated renewed interest in the new investigation. On the night Anne died, it was believed he was in the Ball Inn which was a few hundred yards away from where she was supposed to have caught the bus because a description of a van he drove was provided by a witness. The week before the murder he was in the Ball Inn, drinking brandy and smoking the distinctive Craven 'A' cigarettes, which he kept in a silver case. Police believe he should

The Ball Inn, where a Scottish man was seen drinking brandy a week before Anne's murder and close to the bus stop where she should have caught her bus home. (The author)

be regarded as a significant suspect. With his soft Scottish accent, giving the impression he was possibly from the Inverness region, he called himself Pete, was in his mid-20s, approximately 5ft 7in tall, of slim build, and had dark eyes and short, well-groomed, auburn hair. He wore a ring with a blue coloured stone on the middle finger of his left hand and significantly, he wore cufflinks. He was wearing a dark-green suit, checked shirt, green tie and tan shoes. He gave the impression he was single and he claimed to have lived in both Rotherham and Doncaster. He appeared to be well educated and talked about psychology. Could it be possible that he was a university student or recent graduate? A week before the murder he had been driving a grey-coloured Commer-type 5cwt van. Presumably this was the same Pete whose description and photofit were printed in newspapers in 1964, who drove a dark-grey Mini van and who offered girls who knew Anne a lift. If this was the case, then it is likely that Sam Dunwell was correct and that Anne did know her killer. If he had offered lifts to Anne's friends, then Anne may have trusted him and willingly got into his van.

The Ball Inn held live entertainment on Wednesday evenings with many people travelling from the Sheffield and Doncaster areas. However, on the Wednesday that Anne was last seen alive there was no entertainment in the pub. Could the Scottish man have returned on the night of Anne's murder in order to enjoy the entertainment, and when there was no entertainment taking place have decided to find his own type of sinister excitement?

'This is an extremely significant sighting,' Detective Super-intendent Roper told the media, 'of a man who has not been identified and I appeal for him to come forward.'

The sighting was not investigated fully in 1964 said Detective Sergeant Hickman because of 'the quantity of reports West Riding police received and the difficulties in following them up. Policing was very different at the time.' She added: 'But we are hoping this will be the big breakthrough we have been waiting for and it is important that we trace this man.'

The Scottish man was of particular interest because of the girl believed to be Anne who was seen walking towards a van matching the description of his van, and the knowledge that the driver of that van was wearing shiny cufflinks. The Scottish man had been known about back in 1964 but he was just one of many people in the investigation and there was no reason why he was considered to be of particular interest. It was only when the information was put together decades later that he sprung to the forefront of the detectives' considerations.

'We went back to original statements and found a man who had told the police at the time about the Scotsman. The detail and description we have of this man is incredible, particularly when you consider the passing of time. We think that this man will be known to family and friends in Scotland and could be back living there,' the media was told.

If he had chosen not to wear cufflinks on either occasion that he was seen then perhaps the significance of him would never have been recognised at all.

Detective Sergeant Sue Hickman said: 'Obviously, putting every-thing together we think it's a very strong lead. The description of this man fits everything we have been appealing for before. He was driving the right sort of vehicle and was in the Ball Inn a week before Anne's murder. And there are various things we have been told about him by the witness that make us very interested in this man.' Sadly, however, the police did not fully recognise the significance of this man back in 1964 despite being aware of him at such an early stage in their inquiries. If they had, then Anne's killer may have been brought to justice; if indeed he was responsible. This man would eventually, after 40 years, become the prime suspect in the murder investigation and although details varied in the description of him it is likely it was the same man.

Of course, there is no evidence proving his guilt, with the evidence being purely circumstantial and there being no direct evidence that he was in the area on the night of Anne's death, but he was rightly considered to be a significant suspect. Clearly, though, there were numerous individuals acting suspiciously that night. But the Scottish man remains the prime suspect even though detectives could not conclusively eliminate another of their major suspects. So, Anne's murderer was eventually believed to have been one of two men and it was hoped that if DNA samples could be obtained from them both, the evidence would finally prove which of them was responsible. Both of the suspects were convicted child sex offenders and one had been jailed for murder-ing a girl. Which of these men was the Scottish man could not be established during my research. Unfortunately, DNA from mouth swabs could not be obtained because by the time they had been identified as significant suspects the two men had died, but the police still had hopes that they could obtain some DNA from the men. 'We have DNA samples from Anne's body and we will be matching these with items of clothing belonging to the two men. All we need is a hair, or a trace of sweat left behind on an old hat ... DNA technology gives us the means to find out who murdered Anne,' Roper said. Unfortunately, it appears that either DNA could not be obtained from any items belonging to the men, or if it was, there was insufficient evidence to prove it originated from them. With no DNA from the suspects to compare to that trace found on Anne's clothing the forensic work could progress no further. To potentially get so close, by limiting the number of suspects to just two men, and yet not be able to prove which man was responsible will inevitably have caused tremendous frustration for the team who had carried out a phenomenal investigation.

So ... was the Scottish man or the other suspect responsible for one of South Yorkshire's most shocking crimes or have the police been focussing their attentions on the wrong men, leaving any relatives of each dead man uncertain about whether he was responsible?

Soon after the new murder investigation began in 2002, Detective Superintendent Roper told a press conference that every effort would be made to establish the identity of the killer: 'The investigation will go on until all realistic lines of inquiry have been exhausted,' he said. The police probably know who killed Anne but it appears they have exhausted all available realistic lines of inquiry at this time. It seems likely that as things currently stand the police will not be able to prove with certainty, which of their suspects carried out the awful crime almost fifty years ago. Anne Dunwell's killer took his secret to the grave where it is likely to stay.

CHAPTER 7

The Most Wanted Man in Sheffield: The Hunt for the Killer of John Wortley
(1975)

It was the day when millions in Britain were considering whether to vote 'Yes' or 'No' – but in Sheffield detectives had a more deadly matter to consider.

It was Referendum Day on Thursday, 5 June 1975, with the public given the chance to vote on whether or not Britain should stay in the Common Market – a subject dominating conversations and the media. Also in the Sheffield press that day, was a report on rising crime, with *The Star* quoting an appeal judge who believed that 'fundamental and far-reaching changes are needed in the British penal system to keep down crime.' Crime was an issue which was to dominate the local press for the next few months as armed robberies, sexual assaults, a rape and car thefts occurred in Sheffield. The papers were also to be dominated by a violent murder in the city centre which took place on the evening of polling day.

Realisation that the crime had taken place came when a motorist approached the kiosk on the lower level of the National Car Park (which still stands today, with entry and access points on Pond Street and Arundal Gate). The motorist wanted to pay for parking but was shocked to find the attendant slumped on the floor in a pool of blood. The time was 8.23pm. The police were called and when PC Martin Gourley arrived he realised the man was dead. The victim was quickly identified as John Henry Wortley

John, 66, previously worked at the Neepsend gas station but had retired two years earlier. He then began work as a night attendant

It was in this NCP car park that John Wortley was viciously murdered. (The author)

at the car park as a means of supplementing his pension. It has been reported that on the night of the murder John had been covering for a colleague who was off work due to sickness. John was a married man with three adult children, six grandchildren, and a seventh on its way. At the time of the murder, his wife Jessie was staying in Huntingdon with the couple's daughter having needed a rest after moving house to Frederick Road in the Abbeydale part of the city. John and Jessie were happily married and John was described as a loving family man. As well as his family he loved his Alsatian, Edda. John was said to be a friendly neighbour. One resident in Frederick Road described him as 'a lovely man, as quiet as you could wish. I've never known anyone so quiet. He wouldn't harm a fly.' Whilst the last comment is one attributed to most murder victims – even if the comment is not necessarily accurate – all accounts of John were of a good, honest, caring and friendly man. He used to check on neighbours if he had not seen them for a few days and was a well thought of individual.

　　Why was such a good man killed in such a violent manner? The article relating to the appeal judge's comments about the need to change the penal system had the headline 'Public being bamboozled on crime causes'. Certainly, in the case of the murder of John Wortley there was no doubt about the cause of that crime. He was murdered by an individual or group of people with the motive of robbery in mind. The money collected by John that evening had been stolen. It was believed that the amount would have been between £50 and £70 and would have been largely in silver coins. It may sound an insignificant sum – and certainly it was a small amount for a man's life – but in 1975 most workers were earning between £50 and £60 per week and, of course, large numbers of people were paid significantly less.

The murder weapon was also easily identified by the police. A large bloodstained fire extinguisher was found next to John's body. It was apparent the extinguisher had been the large object used to repeatedly batter the man about the head and inflict the fatal injuries. A post-mortem undertaken by Dr Alan Usher on the night of 5 June confirmed these injuries had been the cause of death.

The media appeals for information began the day after John's murder in an article in *The Star* and also about the referendum result and headlined 'It's Yes to Europe'. The approximate time of the murder, the crime scene location and the motive were all revealed along with an appeal for anyone with information to come forward. 'This is a difficult inquiry and one where we're going to need as much help from the public as possible,' said Detective Chief Superintendent Kenneth Chambers, Head of South Yorkshire CID, who headed the murder inquiry.

The crime scene was quite an ideal place to commit such a murder. It was barely illuminated at night and there were a number of ways of entering and leaving the car park without necessarily being seen. Even in the daytime the lower level, with a kiosk manned by one member of staff, was quite dark in areas. The lower level was scheduled to have closed two hours after John was fatally attacked. The upper level had two members of staff. Following the murder, staff who worked on the lower level voiced their fears of working at night. Staff also told the police and the press that often they would see tramps sleeping in the car park but had not seen them arrive. 'Some strange people come in the park at night and they don't have cars. Gangs of drunken youths often storm through the park,' said John's colleague Muriel Sissons. She and other staff said they did not patrol at night times and tended to stay inside their kiosks which they locked from the inside. There were no security staff, lights or alarms, and of course, in 1975 there were no CCTV cameras. If only staff had expressed their safety concerns prior to the murder then perhaps some measures could have been implemented – if only to have two members of staff working together on all night shifts. As it was, there was only a telephone and a door lock to protect the solitary worker. (The car park attracts trouble makers to this day. I myself have witnessed gangs of youths causing trouble there.)

Prior to John's murder this NCP had been the scene of sexual assaults, car break-ins and car thefts because of the lack of lighting and the many means of escaping without being seen. Perhaps significantly, an attendant had been threatened by a gang of 'thugs' just two weeks before the murder. On that occasion the attendant had stayed inside the kiosk and kept it locked. Eventually the thugs left. Could there have been a connection between this incident and the murder? The police did not seem to think so because they would later concentrate their efforts on trying to identify one man in his thirties or forties, as will soon be discussed.

Although the crime scene was somewhat secluded, the car park was, and still is, in the heart of a busy area on the edge of Sheffield's city centre. Back in 1975 there were bingo halls, a train station, a bus station, clubs, pubs and bars in the vicinity, so there were potentially a large number of witnesses outside of the car park who might have seen something of relevance. These people had to be spoken to in addition to those who had been in the car park that evening.

It has been said that staff working on the lower level locked the kiosk door from the inside during night shifts and did not leave until the end of their shift. Yet John was murdered inside the kiosk, and his body was found inside with the door unlocked. Therefore his killer must have been able to get inside at a time when the door was not locked. The police were mystified as to why the door would have been unlocked. John's widow confirmed he would have kept the door locked. 'He always had the door locked, with the key on the inside,' Jessie Wortley told *The Star*. 'He was very methodical, especially where other peoples' money was concerned.' This was accepted by the police, with Chambers telling the newspaper: 'We know that he kept the kiosk locked. If he let someone in it could be that he knew them. But that is just a theory. We don't know it for a fact.'

The theory that John may have known his killer is a reasonable one. It is quite possible that a man so friendly would have got to know people, especially if they were regular users of the car park. However, there are other distinct possibilities as to why the door could have been unlocked for the killer to enter. Perhaps John went to the toilet and was followed back, with the murderer entering before John managed to lock the door. Another possibility is that there was a fight or some disturbance which John went to intervene in and this led to him being killed and the kiosk robbed. A further possible scenario is that someone pretended there was a fault with their car, or a similar problem which needed assistance, and John innocently went to help and fell into the trap of leaving his kiosk unlocked.

Although John was a caring, non-violent man, his widow believed he would have tried to fight back if he could. There was no sign of any fight or any effort on John's part to defend himself. There were also no raised voices or screams heard which suggests the attack happened suddenly. John was only a short man, just 5ft 4in tall, and weighed only 8st. It is likely he would have been quickly overpowered.

Despite there being a telephone in the kiosk, there was no effort to dial 999 which suggests the killer entered without raising any suspicion – such as being invited in or that it all happened so quickly there was no time for John to make the call.

Given that the murder weapon was a fire extinguisher already located within the kiosk, it is likely the crime was not premeditated. Perhaps John's attacker or attackers had only intended to rob but struck him in order to stop any resistance.

Evidence to support the police's theory of John knowing his killer was in the form of witness sightings of him talking with a man inside the kiosk an hour before the attack. The time of the attack was known to within a few minutes because John had been seen alive at 8.18pm and his body was found at 8.23pm. The man had been seen in the kiosk at between 7.15pm and 7.25pm. Initial descriptions of this man varied tremendously. He was described by one witness as being aged between 30 and 40 years old, 5ft 8in tall, unshaven and with a tanned complexion, rugged features, dark wavy hair and broad shoulders. He was said to be wearing a chequered jacket. However, he was described by another witness as having a dark jacket or brown suit. Another witness said he had dark collar-length hair, and a further witness said he had short light-brown hair. All witnesses believed he was aged between 30 and 45. These differences could be explained by the brief nature of the observations and the poor lighting, but such confusion amongst witnesses made identification of this man difficult.

A photofit was produced based upon the most detailed of the descriptions. It was made widely available through the newspapers and was even shown on television but the man did not come forward. Could this be because he was John Wortley's killer and wanted to get away with murder? Could it be that he did not live in the area and was totally innocent? If so what was he doing in the kiosk? Or could it be that the descriptions were so poor that he did not recognise himself from them?

Everyone who used the car park on the night of the murder was asked to come forward to provide any information they might have and to give detectives a complete picture of peoples' movements there around the time of the attack. This led to dozens of people coming forward which enabled detectives to narrow down the time of the attack to those five minutes between John last being seen alive and his battered body being found. People around the car park, such as those waiting for buses and those on a night out, were also questioned. The night after the murder dozens of officers questioned everyone they encountered in and around the car park to find out if they had any relevant information. In the early days of the investigation 80 detectives and police officers were working full time on the murder hunt. This number rose to 120 to compile information to be scrutinised in the incident room in the gym at West Bars Police Station. Indeed, such was the determination to catch the killer, and the need to maintain high levels of staff, that normal leave was cancelled for those involved in the investigation.

Workers at launderettes were asked to look out for any blood-stained clothing because given the nature of the murder it would have been impossible for the killer to have escaped without heavy bloodstaining on his clothes. Some bloodstained clothing was taken to a launderette in the area but there was no evidence linking it to the crime.

It was reported that a wage slip was found near to the kiosk, but its significance was uncertain. It may just have been accidently

West Bars Police Station in the 1970s where an incident room was set up to investigate John Wortley's murder. (Photograph reproduced from the Picture Sheffield Collection, courtesy of Sheffield Local Studies Library)

dropped by any one of the many innocent drivers or passengers who had used the car park.

Inspector Meadows told the press that the police were making extensive enquiries to the usual types of people who were around at the time, including bus drivers, taxi drivers, people who worked at, and frequented, pubs and clubs, and other known characters in the area. He believed, however, that the investigation was being hampered by the difficulty in publicising the appeal for the man seen with John or for any other information further afield. 'Our biggest problem is people who live outside our area. It is getting them to make the effort to get in touch,' he said.

It was felt that there were still people who had been in the car park that evening who were unwilling to give information despite having not been involved in the crime. Perhaps they thought they might be accused of the crime. Or perhaps they did not want their families to know they had been at the car park that evening. Courting couples, who were known to have frequented the car park, were offered anonymity if they came forward.

A detective told the press: 'The smallest thing may lead us to the killer,' and he appealed for any information, no matter how small.

A large amount of information was forthcoming as a result of the high-profile nature of the investigation and the large number of people who were spoken to. However, one week after the murder the police seemed to be no closer to finding a name for the murderer. In the hope of obtaining relevant evidence directly leading to a conviction, John's employer, NCP, offered a £1,000 reward. The police also decided to stage a re-enactment in the hope of obtaining new witnesses as well as jogging the memories of those who had already provided information. It was hoped that by bringing them back to the crime scene and walking them past the kiosk where a man pretending to be John Wortley was seated, they might recall some further information of use to the detectives which had slipped their minds, or which they had not considered to be worth mentioning.

The re-enactment did help, as did repeatedly speaking to the witnesses, especially those who had seen a man inside the kiosk with John approximately an hour before the murder. Having been asked several times what that man looked like, the witnesses were able to provide a more accurate description of him, or at least the police believed the description was more accurate. By the end of June 1975 the police were able to issue a second photofit image of the man along with a description they believed to be the most accurate one. The man they were searching for was now described as 5ft 8in to 5ft 9in tall with hairy arms and long dark hair greying at the temples. He wore a blue shirt and spoke with a Sheffield accent. I would strongly dispute this description because it differs tremendously from those given earlier in the investigation. This is particularly the case regarding the clothing. How could the later witnesses have described the man as having hairy arms when all the original ones said he was wearing a chequered shirt or a jacket? They could not possibly have seen his arms. Perhaps then there were two separate individuals seen. At first three witnesses described the man, but then two more approached the police and then the description altered. By focusing on one description which was probably an amalgamation of more than one man, the police may have made a mistake.

Two weeks after the murder Superintendent Ernest Middleton said of the 'mystery man': 'We would like him or anyone who thinks they know who he is to come forward.' The following week, under the headline 'The Most Wanted Man in Sheffield' the

Morning Telegraph reprinted the photofit and the description of the man. *The Star* said 'The Hunt Steps up for Murder Mystery Man'. In the following months, several appeals were made for this man to come forward. Yet later, the police began to stress that the man might not have been the killer. 'We have no reason to believe he was involved in the crime in any way,' a spokesman said. If he was truly innocent and uninvolved in the murder, then headlines such as 'Most Wanted Man' would have been enough to put fear into his mind and deter him from coming forward. The police's emphasis that he was not necessarily to be treated as a suspect may have been a way of encouraging him to come forward, but it would not necessarily have subsided any fears he may have had. His identity remains a mystery to this day.

It is quite likely the man was not John Wortley's killer. There were other suspects who received very little police or media attention during the course of the investigation and yet some of them were highly suspicious in their behaviour.

Just days after the murder the police were made aware of four young men in a car which sped away from the crime scene just minutes after John Wortley was killed. It was at around 8.30pm that a brown or beige-coloured Ford Cortina Mark 2 was seen driving fast out of the Murco garage exit of the car park before turning left into Fitzalan Square. The description of only one of the men was given. Sat in the back of the vehicle, he was described as being aged between 20 and 22 years and having Afro style fuzzy hair. This appeared to be an important lead amongst possible suspects, but the police still focussed on the man seen an hour earlier.

Towards the end of June the police appealed in *The Star* for information about the drivers of three cars which had been in the car park on the evening of the murder and who had still not been traced. Unfortunately, there were typing errors in the times given and people had to read *The Morning Telegraph* for accurate information. The driver of the first car sought entered the car park at 2.08pm and left at 7.48pm. The driver of the second car arrived at 3.43pm and left at 7.15pm. The driver of the third car arrived at 6.03pm and left at 7.02pm. Any one – or all three – of these car drivers could have seen the man in the kiosk with John Wortley, and perhaps one of them could have actually been in the kiosk. It is unlikely any of them had been the killer because they had all left before the murder, unless they returned, but they could have had useful information.

In July police began to appeal for the driver of a green 1955 model Hillman Minx saloon, seen close to the crime scene, approximately an hour and a half before the attack, to come forward. At 6.55pm a man was seen crouching next to such a vehicle, giving the appearance that he may have been changing a wheel. He was well built, in his 40s, and wearing a white shirt. There was a woman stood nearby watching, as if she was with the man, to whom police also wished to speak. She was in her 40s, with shoulder-length brown hair and was wearing a cardigan. The police spent a lot of resources trying to trace these two individuals, believing they might have witnessed something relevant to what happened an hour and a half later. The police were aided by the fact there were not many of the 20-year-old cars still on the road. They were quickly able to trace more than thirty of the vehicles and speak to their owners, none of whom had been near the car park on that night.

An anonymous telephone caller contacted the Incident Room claiming that two men were involved in the attack but the information was insufficient to lead to a breakthrough. Too little detail was provided.

When six weeks had passed without any arrests being made, and when public appeals for the mystery man to come forward had met with no response, the police decided that a new strategy was necessary. On 17 July it was announced that detectives were to hold a 'forum' for top detectives from the region to come together to discuss the case. Detective Chief Inspector Robin Herod told

A 1955 model Hillman Minx was seen close to the crime scene an hour and a half before the murder. Detectives were keen to speak to its occupants. (The author's collection)

the press: 'The forum will bring extra experience and brain power to bear on all aspects of our investigation.'

Despite the forum and the many appeals for information in the press, on the radio, television and on the streets, the murder squad was unable to find the evidence they needed to find their killer or killers. By the end of July, press reports showed that South Yorkshire Police were low on manpower and that crime was rising. By concentrating their efforts on the hunt for John Wortley's killer and a small number of sex attackers, other investigations were suffering. It was inevitable that the murder investigation would have to be scaled back.

Unfortunately, the £1,000 reward has yet to be claimed and John Wortley's killer has thus far got away with a violent murder committed for what was a relatively small amount of money. There is a strong likelihood that he is, at the time of writing, still alive. Perhaps he is still living in the South Yorkshire area.

The last words should be given to John's wife, Jessie, who just two days after the crime told the press: 'I hope that my husband's murder haunts the killer for the rest of his life.'

One has to wonder whether his evil crime is in his daily thoughts.

Things may have changed with the West Bars Police Station now closed and currently for sale, but the hunt for John Wortley's killer goes on. (The author)

CHAPTER 8

The Violent Murder of Barbara Young (1977)

On 9 March 1977 *The Star* claimed that South Yorkshire 'has a higher rate of violent crime compared with other offences, than any other police district in Britain.' According to the paper, the national average of violent crimes was 70 for every 1,000 non-violent crimes committed. In South Yorkshire, however, it was 77 violent crimes for 1,000 non-violent ones. Little could the writer of the article have known that only three weeks later an incidence of great violence would take place in a South Yorkshire town, which would cost a young woman her life.

It was a dark evening on Tuesday, 22 March 1977, when Doncaster prostitute Barbara Young was seen entering a dimly-lit passageway off Christ Church Road, close to Netherhall Road which formed part of the Red Light District. (Today, Christ Church Road appears quite respectable, with trees lining the street. The passageway remains dimly lit.) Barbara was accompanied by a man and was seen talking to him as they stood in the passageway. There had been no signs of any danger facing the woman when they stepped foot into the passageway, but just minutes later Barbara was seen staggering along Christ Church Road bleeding heavily from a head wound.

Friends who saw Barbara trying to flee from the town centre passageway approached her, concerned that something untoward had taken place. It was apparent she had been injured but the friends thought she was suffering from a fairly minor facial injury, albeit one which was causing great pain and the loss of a large amount of blood. It was only later, when she had been taken to a friend's home, that the extent of the injuries sustained became apparent, but medical assistance was not sought.

It was in this dimly lit alley in Doncaster that Barbara Young was fatally attacked.
(The author)

When they arrived at the friend's house Barbara was still conscious and she was able to give a basic account of what had taken place. After the pair had entered the passageway, according to Barbara, they had briefly talked before the man viciously hit her in the face. Barbara said she was then knocked to the ground and further beaten around the head before the attacker fled, leaving

Christ Church Street, Doncaster, where Barbara Young was seen staggering after being viciously attacked. (The author)

her injured, badly shaken, but conscious. He took her handbag with him.

By the time the police arrived Barbara had died from her injuries. After being put to bed she had been briefly left. When she was checked upon a little later in the night those who had tried to assist her were horrified to find she had died. A post-mortem carried out on that night of 22 March confirmed that she had died as a result of a massive brain haemorrhage, having had her skull fractured; such was the ferocity of the attack.

The police investigation began in earnest, with seventy police officers and detectives forming a murder squad. They concentrated their efforts on questioning residents living in the immediate vicinity of the crime scene, including those living in houses, boarding houses and bedsits. Lorry drivers staying in local overnight accommodation were also questioned and, as always, routine house-to-house enquiries were undertaken. Through questioning witnesses detectives were able to establish that Barbara's killer was a tall, young and dark-haired male, but this description was so vague that it was hardly likely to be very helpful.

A more detailed description was eventually put together and a police photofit was compiled. This was printed in *The Star*, together with a very small article which could easily have not be seen. It had the headline 'This Man is Wanted after Alley Attack' which could, on the face of it, suggest the article was about a mugging rather than a killing and would not encourage any readers who glance through a paper rather than read every article, from looking beyond the headline. The photofit was based upon a witness description of the man seen with Barbara. He was, according to the witness, aged around 29 and was wearing a suit jacket, white open-necked shirt and blue 'Brutus' narrow-bottomed jeans. Anyone with suggestions as to who the man might be was encouraged to contact the incident room at Doncaster Police Station. The image was printed on a small number of occasions but often without any description, once without any headline and never with the full facts of the incident such as the date of the attack. Unsurprisingly, the police did not receive any credible suggestions as to this killer's identity.

Other prostitutes were interviewed as it was believed they might have known the identity of the killer because they too might have been attacked, received threats, heard rumours or even seen something of relevance. But even though the prostitutes may have been in a position to help, detectives probably did not receive the full amount of information in their possession as there has always been a natural reluctance for prostitutes to speak to the police. This reluctance was greater in 1977 because although prostitution was not a criminal offence, prior to 1982 soliciting for sex was punishable with a prison sentence. Today it is punishable with only a fine. So prostitutes then were unwilling to give information to the police because they could show themselves to be guilty of soliciting for sex and as a result go to prison.

The police tried to locate the missing handbag, which was a large leatherette-type bag with a strap. Despite an extensive search of the area and a public appeal, the bag was never recovered. Whether the killer disposed of it or kept it as a trophy or memento of his crime is unknown. One has to wonder whether there was something in the handbag which the killer wanted. When he fled he would have known that Barbara was still alive and so, unless he panicked after starting his attack, it is possible he never intended to actually kill her but instead wanted to steal from her.

As in all murder investigations the police began to build up a profile of the victim. They knew from the outset that Barbara Ann Young was a prostitute. She was 29 years old and separated from her husband with whom she had two children, one of whom had been fostered. The other lived with her husband. Barbara lived in a caravan at the Happy Day Caravan site in Hartfield, near Doncaster.

A search of the caravan was made in the hope that clues could be found identifying her killer, and to build up a greater picture of the dead woman. A diary was found which contained the names and addresses of more than forty men, at least some of whom were presumed to be clients of Barbara's. The police announced through the media that they would be interviewing each of the men, but made an appeal for anyone who felt their name might be in the diary to come forward rather than wait for detectives to turn up on their doorstep. Detectives spoke to each and every one of the men in the diary and were satisfied none of them was responsible for the fatal attack.

The police murder hunt squad may have been large at the outset, rising to more than one hundred at its peak, but the general determination to catch Barbara's killer seems to have been relatively small for society as a whole, and there can be no doubt that this was because she was a prostitute. Usually when a murder is committed, and the killer's identity is unknown, the local newspaper or newspapers will print prominent and frequent appeals for information. This was certainly the case for John Wortley two years before Barbara's death, when several large articles featured in the local press. However, in the case of Barbara Young articles were somewhat lacking in the local press. Indeed when I was searching through the newspaper archives I failed to spot some of the articles at first because they were so small.

On 24 March the *Morning Telegraph* (a Sheffield daily newspaper of the time) reported that the 29-year-old woman had been found dead. The cause of death and a vague description of the killer were given. Although this small article appeared on the front page of the newspaper it was beneath an article relating to the probable reopening of the Armthorpe fuel plant. The main story was headlined 'Jim's Lib Carries him Home' and related to Jim Callaghan being confirmed as Prime Minister having made an agreement, known as the Lib-Lab pact, to keep the Labour

Government in power. Whilst such a story would naturally have been of major interest across the nation, for a local newspaper the murder of a local woman should surely have been more prominent than a national story that was to be publicised on television and in every other newspaper. Very few newspaper reports relating to the murder followed. *The Star* printed an article the day after the murder stating that Barbara's diary had been found but did not provide the date and time of when the attack was committed. In fact, there were no reports stating the time of the attack which meant that it was less likely to find potential witnesses. The following day the *Telegraph* printed an article stating that the number of police on the investigation might be increased and an appeal was made for anyone who might know the whereabouts of Barbara's handbag. An article in *The Star* on 25 March appealing for information about two men seen in the area was not much bigger than an article relating to the astronomer Patrick Moore (who has no connection to South Yorkshire) being bequeathed a telescope.

On 1 April an appeal was made for information about anyone who had inexplicably left their home or lodgings, who had failed to turn up to work in recent days or had been acting suspiciously. The police confirmed that they were not connecting the murder with an attack on a 33-year-old woman in Thompson Avenue, Edlington, on the previous Wednesday night. On that same day a very small photofit was printed but only below a much larger photograph of a bikini-clad young woman who was wishing readers a 'Happy Easter'. On the same page was a larger article about an FBI probe in the USA into the murders of 20 informants – all when a murder in the newspaper's circulation area received minimal coverage.

An anonymous female caller contacted the police to provide information but due to a technical problem the call was 'foiled' by a bad line and the woman was cut off. On 4 April the police appealed for her to contact them again. If she did, her information did not lead to the breakthrough detectives were seeking.

Other information was forthcoming, however. The descriptions of three men detectives wished to speak to were released. The men were seen in the area at around the time of the attack and were not the same individual upon which the photofit was based. The first was described as being 5ft 9in to 5ft 10in tall, of medium build, aged between 28 and 29, with black neck-length hair, a ruddy complexion, and with acne on his face, especially his chin and forehead. He was seen running from the Christ Church area on the night of the attack. The second man was described as aged between 23 and 25, of slim build, 6ft 1in tall, and with shoulder-length dark hair. The third man was believed to have been delivering seed potatoes in a lorry. He was in his mid-forties, 5ft 3in tall, of medium build and with black hair. He was wearing a boiler suit. The three men were seemingly unconnected to one another. Given that they differed so greatly in appearance to the man seen with Barbara, they must have only been potential witnesses rather than suspects. If any of these men were traced, however, they too were unable to provide detectives with the evidence they needed to catch the killer.

Towards the end of March police obtained a new lead when they learnt that a young man had been seen 'teasing' Barbara hours before the fatal attack. The man was in his early 20s, had dark brown hair and wore a denim suit. The couple were seen outside Hodgson and Hepworths in the Arndale Centre (original name of the Frenchgate Centre) in Doncaster town centre. The nature of the 'teasing' was not disclosed by detectives but one can assume it was an unpleasant incident. Was it a coincidence or could this man have later been involved in an act of violence towards the woman he had been 'teasing'? Although detectives were able to piece together most of Barbara's movements prior to her attack, there was a half-hour period, between 8pm and 8.30pm, for which they could not account. What was Barbara doing during this time, immediately prior to being assaulted? Was she with her killer or with another client?

From April onwards media articles became less frequent and quickly ceased altogether. It could be argued that there was less interest in Barbara's death than in cases where the victim had not been a prostitute.

And yet this was at the time when there was fear across Yorkshire and Lancashire due to the crimes of the Yorkshire Ripper. Peter Sutcliffe's murder spree was in progress between 1975 and 1980, with a 'Ripper' murder having taken place just weeks before the fatal attack on Barbara Young. While the police in the north of the country were searching for a serial prostitute killer it beggars belief that the media did not play its important duty in assisting detectives find a man who murdered one prostitute in the south of

The Frenchgate Shopping Centre in Doncaster where Barbara was seen arguing with a man hours before she was fatally attacked. (The author)

the county. For all they knew there could have been a connection between this South Yorkshire case and the crimes of the Yorkshire Ripper.

With a vague description and an evident hostility towards prostitutes amongst the populace at large – reflected in the media's refusal to give this case adequate publicity – it was almost inevitable that Barbara's killer would get away with murder.

Thankfully, things have changed tremendously in recent years, and *The Star* and other newspapers in South Yorkshire must be praised for their coverage of the unsolved murders of two Sheffield prostitutes whose lives were taken in 1994 and 2001.

Following the conclusion of his trial, South Yorkshire police did question Peter Sutcliffe in relation to this murder because his initial *modus operandi* had been to strike his victims' heads with a blunt instrument. In the year that Barbara Young was killed, Sutcliffe is known to have attacked six women, killing four of them. The questioning failed to uncover any evidence linking Sutcliffe to the murder of Barbara Young. It was, and still is, police practice to question convicted killers who murder strangers in connection

Sutcliffe to be seen on unsolved cases

By Arthur Osman and Richard Ford

Detectives from several forces want to interview Peter Sutcliffe, jailed for life last week after being found guilty of 13 murders, over unsolved murders and attacks in the north of England and Scotland during the 1970s.

Judges reject appeal plea

Ripper's help sought on death riddles

By ROGER CROSS

Newspaper headlines relating to the Yorkshire Ripper being questioned in connection with unsolved murders, including the murder of Barbara Young.
(The author's collection)

with any unsolved murders committed in areas where the killer may have had some connection. Indeed, Sutcliffe was questioned about dozens of murders in which he presumably had no involvement in. When he finally confessed to being the Yorkshire Ripper he gave a full account of his crimes and was willing to confess to those he did commit; an attribute common in serial killers. His refusal to admit to other murders, and the entire lack of evidence linking him to them, suggests he probably was not involved in them. The police were satisfied that he did not play any role in Barbara Young's death.

And so it remains that more than three decades after the savage attack which left a mother dead, the police are no closer to finding her killer.

CHAPTER 9

The Tragic Murder of an Unidentified Baby Girl (1981)

here are few news stories in local news which can generate as many emotions as when a newborn baby is left abandoned in a public place by its mother. Sadly, such an event occurs too frequently. Usually, the mother is identified, located and given any medical and emotional support required. Also, usually the child is given medical help if needed. Unfortunately, in this case neither of these things happened.

It was Tuesday, 22 September 1981, and the newspapers were dominated by the battle between Tony Benn and Denis Healey for deputy leadership of the Labour Party. The SDP was also trying to determine who should lead the newly-founded party. Also in the news that day were stories about unemployment, with the dole queue nearing three million; the news that council tax in Sheffield would be frozen, and a youth remanded in custody for a week for possessing an airgun outside Buckingham Palace.

That same day, a cleaner at the British Home Stores in Cheapside, Barnsley, made a grim discovery when arriving to carry out her duties at the ladies toilet at the restaurant on the third floor of the shop.

Entering the toilet she found a newborn baby girl. This was no ordinary child abandonment, however, because the baby was dead. It was established during a post-mortem that the child had indeed been born alive; most probably on the afternoon of the previous day. It was apparent the baby was already dead when taken into the toilet and had been left there, presumably by the child's mother. Although the newspaper articles of the time did not refer to the case as murder, South Yorkshire police still consider the child to

Cheapside, Barnsley, where a newborn baby was found dead in the British Home Store.
(The author)

have been deliberately killed and the case features in their list of unsolved murders.

Police appealed for the mother to come forward. 'We are very concerned about the mother and want to contact her as soon as possible. She may be in need of medical treatment and we want her to get in touch with us,' a police spokesman was quoted in *The Star* when appealing for information. Unfortunately, other newspapers were less helpful. The *Sheffield Morning Telegraph* printed a 39-word article merely stating that the body of a baby had been found and that police wanted to trace the mother.

Unfortunately, the mother never did come forward and her identity, and thus the identity of the child, remains a mystery. Modern DNA techniques could, however, be used to establish the baby's identity. If the identity of the mother can then be established, and if she was responsible for her child's death, then the mystery of why this crime was committed may finally be resolved.

CHAPTER 10

The Murder of the Cheerful Jamaican: The Calculated Murder of Terivia Cameron (1982)

he killer of Terivia Cameron quite possibly breathed a sigh of relief if he or she chose to read the local news-papers following his wicked crime. Amongst articles including the threat to 2,000 jobs at Sheffield City Council due to government spending cuts and a Sheffield steeplejack who had returned to work after being trapped in a chimney 170ft off the ground for eight hours, there was a small article about his or her own handiwork. The initial press reports stated that the woman had died in a terrible accident at her home. 'Disabled Woman Dies in Flat Blaze' was the headline in *The Star*. The 55 year-old, as she was described in the early reports, died in a blaze in her ground-floor flat at Addy Close in the Upperthorpe area of Sheffield, close to the University of Sheffield's main campus, despite 'frantic rescue attempts'. But the police were not treating the death as suspicious, a police source confirmed. The cause of the fire was being investigated, however, and the coroner Dr Herbert Billing had been informed. It was originally thought that the fire was caused by Mrs Cameron smoking in bed, something which she was known to often do, during which she may have dropped the cigarette or fallen asleep. The police belief that there were no suspicious circumstances was soon to be revised following the post-mortem, and the case would become one of the most shocking murders to be committed in South Yorkshire where the murderer remains at large.

Addy Close, the scene of the cold and calculated murder of a disabled woman.
(The author)

The police refer to the victim as Tervina Cameron but journalists who spoke to her family, friends and neighbours called her Terivia. Due to this uncertainty I shall simply refer to her as Mrs Cameron.

On that day of Thursday 8 July, 1982, it was believed that Mrs Cameron had tried to raise the alarm and get assistance by pressing the emergency buzzer in her flat, but the alarm went unheeded, if indeed it *was* used. At least two neighbours claimed they heard the buzzer but police later doubted that Mrs Cameron had sounded the buzzer herself, believing instead that it must have been the killer pressing the buzzer for some unknown reason, or that a buzzer from another flat was sounded.

The first definite sounds associated with the crime were later described by Brenda McKinnon who had heard frantic banging coming from Mrs Cameron's flat, or a nearby flat. She was uncertain about where the banging originated and put the noise down to children playing noisily. 'I heard a bit of a struggle, some tumbling and a big crash. I thought it was the children and thought no more of it. If Mrs Cameron needed any help she used to bang on the wall,' said Brenda McKinnon.

A mumbled voice, which was later interpreted as a cry for help, was also heard but was not loud enough to distinguish anything was seriously wrong. It was not until the flames spread and the fire was seen that the neighbours began to act. Brenda's daughter Jacqueline, who knew Mrs Cameron well, often ran errands for her and spent time keeping her company, later reflected on the incident. 'I would have gone to help and even if I could not have helped I could have got somebody else to rescue her. We just did not know what was happening. I feel really terrible.'

The situation first became apparent when flames and smoke were seen by Irene Buxton as she was cleaning her windows. Her 18-year-old son Tim and 30–year-old Stephen Jamieson smashed a window of the flat to gain entry. They battled through thick black smoke and found Mrs Cameron lying unconscious on the floor beside her bed. By this time Brenda and Jacqueline Mckinnon had also seen the smoke and joined the rescue, dragging Mrs Cameron by her legs into the hallway but they could not get her out of the flat because of the smoke and flames. Stephen's wife, Ann Jamieson, described the scene and the difficulties the rescuers faced. 'Mrs Cameron didn't walk very well. I tried to get in the flat but the smoke was terrible. It was pretty well alight,' she said.

Other neighbours tried to put the fire out by pouring buckets of water over the flames but it was too intense and widespread. It was believed that approximately two hundred people were at the scene trying to assist or watching in horror as events unfolded.

Firefighters from the Division Street fire station rushed to the scene to extinguish the fire and try and save Mrs Cameron's life after removing her from the building. They used a resuscitator, believing that Mrs Cameron may have been overcome by smoke inhalation, and gave her heart massages. She was taken to the Royal Hallamshire Hospital but was pronounced dead on arrival.

It would later be shown that it would not have mattered if the rescuers had acted more quickly once the fire had started and if medical help had been given sooner, because Mrs Cameron was already dead.

The truth was announced on 10 July on the front page of *The Star* beside an article relating to a blazing Pan-American World Airways jet which had crashed after take off in New Orleans, killing 145 on board and at least four people on the ground. In addition to this story, readers were told that the 'defenceless crippled pensioner' had in fact been murdered. A post-mortem was undertaken by Home Office pathologist Dr Alan Usher who revealed that Mrs Cameron had not died of smoke inhalation as she had not been breathing at the time when smoke was being produced. This had not been an accident and it was not even a case of an arson attack in which someone had been trapped inside the building. Instead, Mrs Cameron had been strangled by some-one's bare hands prior to the fire being lit. Afterwards, the flat had been set fire to, with fires being started in at least two areas of the flat. The bed in particular was almost totally destroyed by the flames.

The news shocked Mrs Cameron's neighbours who were already trying to cope with the fact a fire had taken place and their neigh-bour and friend had died. 'It was terrible thinking she had died in the fire, but it is even worse knowing she was murdered,' Brenda Mckinnon told *The Star*. For Mrs Cameron's relatives, however, it was even worse because rather than hearing from the police that their loved one had been murdered, they learnt the shocking truth from the television news.

The murder investigation began in earnest with one hundred police and detectives hunting the killer from the outset. Detective Superintendent David Chapman, who led the investigation from an incident room at Hammerton Road Police Station in the Hillsborough area of the city (the police station where a year earlier Peter Sutcliffe was questioned and where he made his lengthy confession for his murders), said: 'Mrs Cameron was killed by a callous, cold-blooded murderer. The calculated way it was carried out speaks for itself. We are now satisfied the fire was started deliberately and there was more than one seat of the fire.' He gave his personal assurance of granting anonymity to any informant who provided the crucial information to catch the killer.

It was clear the murderer had deliberately lit the fire to destroy evidence and also possibly in the hope of making the authorities believe that Mrs Cameron had died through an accidental fire rather than through strangulation. Exactly how long before the fire was set that Mrs Cameron was strangled, is unknown.

To kill such a frail woman in her own home, in such a manner, and then set fire to the flat showed detectives that they had a cunning killer to catch and they immediately recognised the challenges they faced. Forensic evidence at the scene would have been difficult to obtain because the majority of it would have been destroyed, and forensic techniques were a shadow of what they are today (DNA testing was still something of the future). The best hope of finding vital clues was to speak to any witnesses who may have seen someone or something of relevance.

The fire itself drew, as has been said, large numbers of people to the scene. It was hoped these people might possibly be important witnesses. 'Obviously they were attracted by all the activity of the firemen, and it was an enormous number of people to interview to see what information they had,' Chapman told the press. In all likelihood, however, the killer would have been long gone by the time the attention of the neighbours was attracted.

A woman and young child were seen speaking to Mrs Cameron hours before the fire began. The conversation had taken place through a window in the flat at around 1.45pm. The woman was described as being aged around 50 years old, of 'plump' build, 5ft 7in tall, with short light brown hair and wearing a dark cardigan. The child was described as being a nine or 10-year-old boy with blond hair, who was wearing yellow trousers.

Rod Jones from South Yorkshire Police told the press: 'They could have been the last people to see Mrs Cameron alive and could have vital information. We want to hear from them and anyone who knew her. We have to build up a picture of her life and every piece of information helps.'

By speaking to Mrs Cameron's neighbours, friends, relatives and fellow churchgoers, the police were able to build up a picture of the victim. Terivia Matilda Cameron was born in Jamaica and had moved to Britain in the late 1950s. She had worked for several years as a nurse at Middlewood Hospital but had been forced to leave her job after suffering from a major stroke. She had once lived with her sister but had to move into her specially-adapted flat where she was more able to live an independent life and she lived there alone. It was uncertain exactly how old she was, with reports giving her age as anything between 55 and 60. Later articles described her more consistently as being 60 years old and that was probably her correct age. Known to friends as Terry, she was very popular and well-liked by those who knew her. She was always laughing, they said, and she was known as 'the cheerful Jamaican'. Mrs Cameron regularly visited the Kelvin Day Centre. She attended church every Saturday when she would be collected, have lunch and stay the day with her church friends. She was also frequently visited by the pastor and they would sing songs together and read the Bible.

Mrs Cameron had been determined to beat the effects of the stroke which had left her severely disabled. Her cousin, Barbara Coburn, told the press: 'She always believed she would get better. She talked about it all the time and worked hard to get back the feeling she had lost after her stroke.' Mrs Cameron was able to walk with difficulty, using a stick and visited shops locally when she could; trying to lead as normal a life as possible, but the effects of her illness had left her very frail. This made the crime against her all the more shocking. Another cousin, Vernon Solomon, said that the former nurse had been 'absolutely dedicated to her work and her records will testify to that. Her illness came as a terrible blow.'

Mrs Cameron's daughter, Dorothy Bailey, and her grandson flew from Canada to grieve for her mother and to appeal for information about the person who took her life.

The crime was believed to have been motivated by money. It was thought perhaps Mrs Cameron had been the victim of a robbery which went horribly wrong. One of her neighbours, Stephen Hale, told the media that Mrs Cameron was known to have a lot of money in her flat. 'She kept a lot of money in her blanket chest in her bedroom because she couldn't get out to go to the bank,' he said. It was alleged by Mrs Cameron's friends and her cousin that she had been robbed of more than £4,000 approximately three months prior to her death. If this was true, and the police tried to confirm the story, then robbery was a likely explanation because it is a fact that once a home is burgled it increases the chances of a second burglary being committed. A person who had robbed Mrs Cameron once would have felt confident in doing so again in the knowledge that substantial sums of money were kept on the premises, that the victim was vulnerable, and that security was lax. Also, amongst burglars and other such criminals it is well known that information is traded relating to which properties are worth targeting. However, detectives were unable to ascertain what, if anything, had actually been stolen, although there was no trace of the pension money which she had drawn just three days before her death. Even if nothing had been stolen it does not mean there was no intention to commit robbery.

The media responded well to police appeals for information, producing major stories in the hope that important clues could be obtained from the public. In a large front page article on 12 July *The Star* appealed for anyone who saw Mrs Cameron on the day she died to come forward and help build up a complete picture of her movements that day, which were still a mystery for the detectives working on the case.

Detectives were keen to speak to anyone who had seen Mrs Cameron at the small Upperthorpe shopping area, located only a short distance from her home, on the day of the fire. They visited the shopping area to speak to people in order to investigate the theory that the dead woman may have been there hours before her death. Mrs Cameron had been seen walking with a woman towards Addy Drive at around 10.30am. The police needed to speak to this woman and also the woman seen with a child talking to Mrs Cameron three and a quarter hours later. 'We have still not heard from these people and want them to come forward,' Chambers said. 'We have to build up a picture of her movements and they could have vital information. However unimportant it may seem to them it could be of great importance to us.'

With the killer not having been identified after a week of investigations, a massive police operation was launched. The estate was sealed off to ensure as many people as possible could be spoken to. At dawn on 15 July, officers began standing at every street corner with the intention of speaking to everyone who walked along the streets. There were seven entrances to the estate and each one of them had officers in position. A poster campaign was also launched, with large billboards showing a photograph of Mrs Cameron along with an appeal for information. Three questions were asked on the posters: Were you in this area on that date? Did you see this woman? Did you see the house fire at Addy Close? Police questioned residents and other passers-by, until 8.35pm that night.

As a result of the cordon the 'plump' woman who had been accompanied by the child was located. She was spoken to about her conversation with Mrs Cameron, her own movements that day and what she may have seen. The woman was unable to offer any useful information.

More than one thousand homes were visited during police house-to-house enquiries. Approximately one hundred detailed statements were taken. At the time, the hunt for Mrs Cameron's killer was the largest seen in the city in recent years, with 125 officers in the murder squad at the height of the investigation.

Detective Superintendent Chambers praised his officers for their hard work, which saw them working a minimum of twelve hours a day. He said: 'We have an excellent team of high calibre officers. They are determined to find out who committed this murder.'

Chapman reiterated his own commitment to solve the case and 'put the strangler behind bars'. He added: 'We will continue these investigations however long it takes to bring them to a satisfactory conclusion.' Perhaps significantly the woman seen walking with Mrs Cameron did not come forward. Was this because she feared false accusations against her if she was innocent or could she have been involved? Or was Mrs Cameron killed by another individual whose presence in the area went unnoticed?

On 20 July Mrs Cameron was laid to rest at the City Road cemetery in Sheffield. As a sign of her popularity and the public horror at the horrific murder of a disabled woman, almost two hundred mourners packed into the Seventh Adventist Church on Andover Street, Pitsmoor, for the funeral service. Amongst the congregation were a number of detectives who not only wished to pay their own respects, but who wanted to pick up clues from the behaviour of those present or overhear any suspicious remark. The service was led by Pastor Peter Sayers who, in his eulogy, described Mrs Cameron as a loving mother. 'Hers was a short life, too short. She was the salt of the earth, the light of the world.' He added, 'It was a privilege to know her. Despite her terrible affliction she kept her faith and was an inspiration to us all.'

On the day of the funeral a more recent photograph of the victim was released to the press and used in appeals. It was very different from earlier photographs and showed Mrs Cameron with spectacles and a different hairstyle. 'We are progressing forward in a very positive manner,' Chapman told the press. 'There are no fresh leads but we have accumulated a tremendous amount of information which is being examined with a fine tooth comb.' He expressed his frustration about a number of conflicting accounts from witnesses relating to Mrs Cameron's movements on the day she died which had hindered the investigation.

The police stepped up the investigation further, but as July came to an end the identity of the person who took Mrs Cameron's life

City Road cemetery where Mrs Cameron was laid to rest. (The author)

in such a violent manner was still as much a mystery as it had been three weeks earlier. By 30 July approximately 8,000 people had been spoken to by detectives hunting the killer, two thousand front doors had been knocked on and approximately four hundred detailed statements had been taken. The police were still keen to speak with anyone who could say for certain that they had seen Mrs Cameron shopping on the day of her death. A number of people had thought they had seen her but they were not completely sure. By this time 80 detectives and officers were working on the investigation, sifting their way through what was described as a 'mountain' of paperwork, but they felt confident they would crack the case.

No one was known to have had any hatred or grudge against the friendly pensioner and there was still no certain motive for the crime despite the strong suspicions of robbery.

Interestingly, eight months after Mrs Cameron's murder a 56-year-old woman named Patricia Hurst was battered to death in her home during a burglary. The home on Ecclesall Road in Sheffield was then set ablaze. A 25-year-old woman and her 17-year-old boyfriend were both arrested and charged with murder.

Following two trials the pair were formally acquitted. The woman was, however, convicted of arson and her boyfriend was convicted of robbery. The case was closed. But it needs to be asked whether there could have been some connection between the two crimes which were committed in the same city and within a relatively short space of time.

'It is a fair assumption that the killer's identity is somewhere among all the information we have gathered,' Chapman said, still believing that a breakthrough in the hunt for Mrs Cameron's murderer was likely. 'We are getting closer to a successful conclusion all the time.'

If indeed the killer's identity *was* amongst the information detectives had gathered, they certainly never found it and their belief that they were getting closer to a successful conclusion was misguided. More than thirty years after one of Sheffield's most horrifying murders, Terivia Cameron's killer, if he or she is still alive, remains at large.

CHAPTER 11

Out of the Cold in South Yorkshire

The work of detectives investigating old unsolved murders, or cold cases as they are more commonly known, has been depicted in popular culture by television dramas such as *New Tricks* and *Waking the Dead*.

The investigation of cold cases by police forces across the country is often successful. During the writing of this book two of the members of the gang responsible for killing black teenager Stephen Lawrence in London in 1993 were convicted of his murder. The convictions followed tremendous public criticism against the police which resulted in a determination to jail those responsible. But improved forensic techniques also made it possible to obtain the proof needed to link the two men to the attack almost nineteen years earlier.

There are, however, cases which have been solved after a greater length of time. In 1979 Teresa de Simone was strangled to death outside a public house in Southampton, Hampshire. The case resulted in the conviction of Sean Hodgson, who was 15 years old at the time and who had previously confessed to several crimes which he was not involved in. In 2009 Hodgson was proven, by DNA evidence, to be innocent of the murder 30 years earlier. The same technology which exonerated Hodgson was used to link another man to the murder. David Lace confessed to raping and murdering Simone but he was not believed on account of a man having already been convicted of the murder. Lace committed suicide in 1988 but DNA tests on his buried remains were consistent with the DNA found on clothing worn by the victim when she was raped and killed. Had it not been for improvements in DNA examination Hodgson would remain in prison and the true killer's identity would be unknown even though he admitted his crime.

In 1975 Joan Harrison was murdered in Preston, Lancashire. Her body was found in a derelict garage two days after she was last seen alive. She had been sexually assaulted and violently killed. The case is best known for the infamous Weirside Jack tape which was sent to detectives hunting the Yorkshire Ripper. On the hoaxed tape, and in letters, the man posing as the Ripper claimed he had killed Joan. There were doubts about a link between the Yorkshire Ripper murders and Joan Harrison's death, but the tapes and letters were accepted by George Oldfield – who originally led the hunt for Peter Sutcliffe – as coming from the Ripper. The tape and letters were only proved to be a hoax following Sutcliffe's arrest and sensational confession. It was not until 2010 that the police identified Joan's killer. During a cold case review, DNA evidence was found on clothing worn by Joan when she was murdered. It was found to match Christopher Smith, whose DNA had been obtained two years earlier when he was arrested for a drink-driving offence. Unfortunately, six days after being arrested for this offence Smith died. However, shortly before his death, racked with guilt, he wrote a three-page letter confessing to his crime.

The above case bears some similarities to the case of Lorraine Jacob who was murdered in Liverpool in 1970. Despite a major investigation the case went unsolved until 2008 when a letter was found in the home of Harvey Richardson who had died days earlier. The letter had been written several years earlier and formed a detailed confession to the murder. It was kept in a box along with a pair of knickers proven by forensic testing to have belonged to Lorraine Jacob, press cuttings relating to the murder, a press cutting to a second unsolved murder (that of Jacqueline Ansell-Lamb who was also murdered in 1970) and an old pistol.

By October 2009, 130 cold cases had been solved across Britain, including murder and sex crimes, although as in the above examples many of those responsible had escaped justice in their lifetimes. However, a large number of criminals have been imprisoned for crimes which they must have believed they had managed to get away with and detectives in South Yorkshire have shared in some of these successes.

The South Yorkshire Cold Case Review Team was founded in 2007 by Detective Superintendent Richard Fewkes, who originally ran the unit. The team was established predominantly to investigate sexual offences, but there is also a programme to investigate unsolved murders. The team of six serving and retired detectives brought back into service to bring their past experience, was originally based at Maltby Police Station but is now based at the Callflex Building in Rotherham and headed by Detective Superintendent Colin Fisher.

There are currently 26 unsolved murders which are within the remit of the review team, the earliest of which is the murder of Lily Stephenson in 1962. Each of these cases is on a two-year rota for review.

In response to a Freedom of Information Act request I made during the writing of this book I was told: 'No undetected murder is ever closed no matter how old. All cases are actively investigated whilst ever there are reasonable/practical lines of enquiry, however long that may be. If new information (of any potential value) comes to light, then this is investigated. All cases are reviewed when time allows, however priority has to be given to current cases and "old cases" are prioritised, i.e. the potential danger to the public the unidentified offender may pose. The likelihood of the offender being dead would of course reduce the position of the case on the "priority" but this is not a reason to close the case forever. The relatives of the deceased deserve to know the truth, if/when it is within our ability to provide such answers.'

Reviews consist of another look at all available documentation from the original investigation. Old police files are gone through with a fine toothcomb in the hope that a fresh pair of eyes may see new potential areas of investigation. Each case typically has police files filling between thirty and forty boxes. However, in some cases the files have been destroyed or lost. In these cases the police have to resort to newspaper archives (with some inevitable errors in reporting) and often using local studies libraries in much the same way as I did during the research of this book.

Witnesses have to be traced and they are spoken to again to verify the information contained in their original statements and to establish if they have any further information which they could not recall at the time, or they did not include in their statements for any other reason. Trained family liaison officers speak with relatives of the victim to keep them fully informed and as involved as possible in the review. Great care has to be taken to ensure the relatives do not have their hopes and expectations raised unduly. If the review fails to make any breakthrough and has to be scaled back once again, the family are, according to South Yorkshire Police, consulted and are 'part of that process' which sees the review ending.

Monthly meetings between the review team and forensic scientists take place to establish how cases can be progressed. Work with these scientists is undertaken to obtain traces of forensic evidence which could link a suspect to a crime. Thankfully, such evidence has been well preserved for most cases.

As part of the forensic review a detailed examination of exhibits associated with a crime, such as a weapon or clothing from the scene (especially the victim's clothing) is undertaken in the hope of finding DNA which may belong to the killer or killers. In murder cases where there is a sexual element then there is a good chance that the murderer's DNA would be present. Also, if there was a struggle during which the victim scratched their attacker, DNA traces could be present and these can survive even after many years. It is a rule of forensic science that every contact leaves a trace, and with improved techniques there is often a high possibility of obtaining forensic evidence which would not have been identifiable from the time of the crime which can now be analysed. Even the tiniest traces of semen, blood, saliva, sweat (such as from a fingerprint or on clothing), skin or hair, can all be used to link a killer to their crime.

In times gone by, forensic evidence was collected using sticky tape to take hair and fibres which may have originated from an attacker from a victim's clothing. The tape often still survives and its hair can be examined.

In the case of clothing which may contain traces of semen, stained areas are cut out and soaked in chemicals to extract sperm cells which can then have DNA extracted. This is usually done with a technique known as Low Copy Number (LCN) DNA analysis which effectively replicates a small number of cells (or even one cell) to produce enough DNA to provide a useful sample for comparisons with the DNA from suspects. The LCN DNA technique can also be used for DNA from other sources.

As a consequence of the DNA technology and techniques established by the Forensic Science Service (FSS), police forces across the country have been undertaking reviews in the hope of obtaining

DNA which can then be compared with that of suspects in order to eliminate them. When a trace of DNA is present a profile can be obtained within nine hours.

In 1995 the FSS set up the National DNA database in Birmingham to allow traces of DNA found at a crime scene to be compared with those on record of a known or suspected criminal. Whilst the database has been controversial there can be no doubt that it has been an important tool in solving cold cases and could be valuable in solving some of the cases featured in previous chapters. Even those cases where DNA has not been found in the past there is the possibility that any future improvements could lead to DNA being obtained. In 2010 there were more than four million records in the DNA database, although many of these were duplicate records.

Since 2004, familial searches have led police to killers and rapists by allowing forensic scientists to establish that DNA from a crime scene is very similar to the DNA of a known individual, which can suggest that the person being sought is a close relative of the person whose DNA is on record.

In 2009 a new technique called DNABoost was first used. The technique separates DNA from different sources which overlap one another on an exhibit. For example, a knife used in a murder might contain the DNA of a victim, the killer and possibly the DNA of others who were completely uninvolved in the crime. Prior to DNABoost it would usually have been impossible to obtain a DNA profile of each individual because there was a mixture of the sources.

Other recent improvements in DNA technology have ensured that only one match in a billion is an error.

These advances in DNA technology and expertise have been taken advantage of by the Cold Case Review Team in South Yorkshire. The team has solved one murder from the 1970s, but the majority of its successes has been securing the evidence to convict those guilty of sex crimes. A total of 105 years of jail sentences were given as a result of the team's work by October 2010.

Brian Wright was convicted of raping a young woman at knife point at the bus station on Pond Street, Sheffield in 1977. Modern DNA techniques were used during a cold case review and Wright's guilt was established. He had been a suspect at the time but his mother gave him a false alibi and the trail went cold. This time he pleaded guilty to the offence and was sentenced to six-and-a-half years in jail.

Christopher Sykes was convicted of raping a 16-year-old girl in Canklow, Rotherham in 1981. A review in 2009 found a trace of DNA which, when run through the DNA database, led detectives to Sykes, who pleaded guilty.

A man who changed his name to Joshua the High Priest was jailed for raping two women in 1984 and 1985. Detectives had not linked the two cases at the time but a review in 2007 found DNA proving both women were attacked by the same man. The DNA matched that in the DNA database and the culprit was brought to justice.

In 2010 Simon Murcott was convicted of a rape he committed in 1985 after a review obtained his DNA profile. When it was run through the DNA database it matched Murcott.

The above criminals would have got away with their crimes if the cases were not reviewed in recent years. This shows the importance of the Cold Case Team but also shows the potential for solving murders, especially sex murders.

The technology at the disposal of forensic scientists, and the results used by detectives is great but there are problems ahead which will reduce the access to the tools to solve cases.

In 2012 the Forensic Science Service was closed down despite its pivotal role in solving more than 220 cold cases and providing 60 per cent of the forensic services used by police forces in England and Wales. The Crime Reduction Minister James Brokenshire announced that the state-funded organisation was costing approximately £2m per month and so would become a victim of austerity cuts. A report published in 2011 stated: 'Our firm ambition is that there will be no continuing state interest in a forensics provider by March 2012. There is no justification for the uncertainty and costs of trying to restructure and retain the business.' It was promised that arrangements would be put in place to provide a supply of forensic work in the future and that 'the continued provision of effective forensics is our priority'. The police have had to pledge their determination to cut costs of forensic work which will add pressures to cold case reviews. This has the probable outcome of little resources being spent on older cases which will be viewed as a lower priority.

It could be argued that solving murders and sex crimes has been affected by the spending cuts of a Government which has put a price on justice

Whilst the latest forensic technology, expertise and techniques can, and does, help solve cases, especially murders where sex has featured, there is not always forensic evidence available in historic murder cases. If there was no close contact between a killer and victim – for example in a shooting – there may not be any forensic trace left at the crime scene which can be used to connect a suspect with the crime. Forensic evidence may also have been lost, contaminated or destroyed between the time of the crime and any cold case review.

When evidence was collected years ago, it was without the expectation that future forensic techniques could be used to analyse it. As such, it was not always handled and stored with sufficient care to reduce the risks of contamination.

The occasional lack of forensic evidence from the scene is not the only problem which can be encountered. Even if a suspect is identified through forensic means or otherwise, the prospects of bringing them to justice are not always guaranteed.

Even when a trace of forensic evidence is found when examination of exhibits is undertaken it does not of course mean that a suspect will be identified. When run through the National DNA Database there might not be any match. The killer's DNA will not be on record if they have not been arrested or convicted of any offence since the creation of the database in 1995. As such, their DNA will only be compared to that from the murder scene if they are identified as a potential suspect. If they never featured in the original investigation, and so were not asked to give a mouth swab, then there may be no comparisons made. Familial DNA could be used but if the killer does not have any relatives on the database then this will also draw a blank.

The passage of time can result in evidence, both forensic and documentary, being lost. Witnesses are not always still alive by the time a suspect is arrested. If they are still alive they may be too ill to testify or they might have little or no recollection of events and so cannot be cross examined in court.

An example of this problem involved a 70-year-old man who had been charged with a murder in 1961. During a cold case review in 2008 Anthony Hall, who was already serving a life sentence for the murder of Sylvia Whitehouse in 1969, was identified as prime suspect in the murder of 15-year-old Jacqueline Thomas. Jacqueline was strangled and sexually assaulted after leaving a fair. Her body was found a week later on an allotment near her home in Bordesley Green. When the case progressed to court, Judge Frank Chapman said that there could be no trial because the murder was 'just too long ago'. He argued that some witnesses were dead, others could not be traced, some were too ill to attend court and the rest would be unable to accurately recollect the relevant information. He added that some evidence and police records had been lost. Judge Chapman said: 'I am aware of the strong public interest in bringing a killer to justice. I am aware that this must be the very last chance to bring someone before a court for the death of Jacqueline Thomas, but I must not let these pressures compound one injustice on another. In my view any trial which was to follow, in this case, would not be balanced and fair.' Following this ruling a member of the West Midlands Major Crime Review Team announced that they respected the court's decision and that they were not looking for anyone else in the investigation. Nonetheless the case remains officially unsolved.

Yet despite the major difficulties in bringing killers to justice there is a determination amongst the detectives in the Cold Case Review Team to find the evidence to secure a conviction to bring closure to the families of the victims before more killers take their secrets to the grave.

Index